CREATIVE SPACE

CREATIVE SPACE

URBAN HOMES OF ARTISTS AND INNOVATORS

FRANCESCA GAVIN

PHOTOGRAPHY BY ANDY SEWELL

LAURENCE KING PUBLISHING

LAURENCE KING

Published in 2009 by
Laurence King Publishing Ltd.
361–373 City Road
London EC1V 1LR
United Kingdom

Tel: +44 20 7841 6900
Fax: +44 20 7841 6910
email: enquiries@laurenceking.co.uk
www.laurenceking.co.uk

A catalogue record for this book is available from
the British Library.

ISBN: 978 1 85669 588 6

Design: MARC&ANNA
Photography: Andy Sewell

Printed in China

BARCELONA
BERLIN
LONDON
NEW YORK
PARIS
TOKYO

CONTENTS

INTRO-DUCTION

IF ONE STYLE DEFINED THE END OF THE TWENTIETH CENTURY, IT WAS MINIMALISM. HANDS DOWN, BLANK WHITE SPACE WAS THE WINNER. ASPIRATIONAL MAGAZINES WERE FILLED WITH 'GLAMOROUS' HOMES THAT LOOKED MORE LIKE ART GALLERIES THAN DOMESTIC SPACES. IT WAS THE ERA OF FENG SHUI, JOHN PAWSON, LOFT-LIVING AND SCANDINAVIAN SIMPLICITY. PEOPLE DAYDREAMED ABOUT ZEN-LIKE SPACES AND CLEAN LINES. BUT SOMEONE FORGOT TO POINT OUT THAT WHITE CUBES ARE BORING.

Who wants to fantasize about remodelling their bathroom? Minimalism is mainstream – something that can be created at Ikea at bargain prices. Blank space with clean lines is an easy aesthetic choice for those lacking in creative imagination. This image is the definition of conformity – now becoming as old-fashioned as wood panels and gilt. In contrast, those pushing underground culture are creating a new interior ideal. What do the homes of artists, designers, curators, writers, photographers, set designers, filmmakers and illustrators look like?

These are homes that reflect the creative process. Places that are a bit rough around the edges, a bit more inventive and spontaneous. Interiors filled with post-modern pop collectables, vintage junk finds, toy collections, underground art, odd objects, handmade things. Places that are an innovative antidote to the sterility of minimalism. One way to define this new way of living is 'creative chaos'.

These are spaces that reflect and inspire creativity. There has always been a fascination with how creative people live, since Alberti and Vasari started documenting artists' lives back in the Renaissance. Creative people's spaces provide a glimpse into creative thought. Their homes give an insight into their work – how they collect inspiration and how their work influences the space around them. It adds another layer to understanding their art.

These domestic spaces also provide a deeper look into the real soul of different international cities; a way to decipher the nuances that make Berlin, Berlin or Tokyo, Tokyo. There are themes that run throughout the homes in this book. There are many different interpretations of collections and modes of display. Found objects and oddities can be discovered in most homes. The little fetishes that people choose to surround themselves with reflect their lives, the influx of imagery and information. There is something excessive about the spaces.

Another reason why these homes are so interesting is that these spaces are not all about flaunting wealth. Sometimes the most inventive homes are the most DIY; the least expensive. These spaces are an alternative to blanket, mindless consumerism. There is almost a political element in denying the aesthetic choices of the mainstream. Why buy when you can create?

Our fascination with interiors reflects a desire to form and define our identity. Private lives are often very different from public personae. Alain de Botton argues lucidly in *The Architecture of Happiness* (2006) how our interiors remind us of who we want to be, how we want to live, our desired projection of self. The world's creative people provide an alternative to the obsession with fame and wealth that dominates modern life. Their lives are an inspiring antidote to vacuous celebrity. They actually make things. They champion individuality. They are simply cool.

Lucio Auri

**ARTIST
FURNITURE DESIGNER
BERLIN**

LOCATION
PRENZLAUER BERG
WWW
lucio-auri.net

AN ART OF IMPROVISATION – MAKING DO BY MAKING THINGS

Lucio Auri's work refuses to be pigeonholed as furniture design or sculpture. He often uses found furniture in his cupboard and shelf installations, which are both functional and conceptual. The Berlin-based artist has also turned his hand to painting, lecturing and interiors. Auri has lived in his flat for a decade. He chose it because he was living around the corner and wanted to keep his phone number. The space – which has the same eclectic colour palette as his sculptural work – is filled with weird and wonderful items discovered on the city's streets.

How did you start?
[I began] drawing cartoons, caricatures of friends and family, designing layouts and cover assignments for fellow students. I always had a sort of hands-on approach to creativity. I made my own toys and accessories, and architectural models.

How and why did you start using found materials in your furniture?
I am not really consciously ethically recycling. I do hate waste though, so it's rewarding finding a creative use for unwanted material. I would say it is more an economic decision to try to find interesting and cheap materials for my work. I also get a lot of inspiration from found objects and materials with a narrative concept or story behind them. Walking through urban wastelands, seeing things I couldn't have and making them how I wanted them to be. That's how I started. An art of improvisation – making do by making things.

What interests you about Berlin?
The empty holes in the fabric, the 100 places in between, the ricochets of history, the bullet holes of memories, the new cracks in creativity. It's a cheap place to live and full of potential. The city doesn't seem to be finished. There are also the different definitions of modernism in this city; socialist iconography versus the Western capitalist logos and vocabularies. All the discarded objects and interventions between East and West. The amazing history and stories within this city.

Tell me about the apartment.
We live on the first floor, the Bel Etage, of a building built in the late nineteenth century. Almost all the rooms have elaborate stucco work in them, ranging from the New Empire look to Italian eclectic. The back of the apartment (the servants' quarters) has honed-down minimal painted decorations. We took a lot of walls out towards the entrance, creating a type of open American kitchen, and pulled down all the false ceilings – which would have hung there to retain the heat in former Eastern Bloc times. We've renovated practically all of the apartment, except the electrics, so at times things do tend to crack and flash during lightning storms.

What is the story with the ceiling mural?
The painting depicts three energetic-looking cherubs hovering with ribbons and floral garlands in a kind of atmospheric entanglement of cloud bodies and decorative masses, all encircling a ceiling rose of ornate plasterwork. And the heavenly bodies have all been censored! Mainly the genitalia. I think the painting is actually quite kitsch… When we first moved into the apartment, it was a right shambles. I always suggested that there was something underneath the rough lime-painted ceiling, but had no intention of restoring it. We were busy enough with electrics and plumbing. Over the years, however, the ceiling kept on peeling and flaking away, even crumbling down onto guests' plates and dishes. It was all a sort of one-night discovery.

Where do you find the objects that fill your home?
Using a storyteller's quotation, 'Between the hearth and the cosmos… home and identity'. I look in a lot of flea markets and garage sales, either around Berlin or where I touch down in the world. Small out-of-the-way shops and alleyways, street markets, second-hand shops. Some things I make.

What are some of the small objects around your space?
Bullroarers, Swiss marital mask carvings, hobo whittle art, scrimshaw odds and ends, handheld souvenirs, offbeat market handicrafts, new-world flotsam and jetsam, tokens from friends and neighbours, discarded seedlings, the forgotten behind-the-shelf analogies, old favourites and tactile disciplines in arts and crafts. I like the household plants, as they have all been found discarded or abandoned, thrown out of windows or blown over third-floor balconies in storms. I have nurtured them to be real exotics and tenacious indoor bastards. The furnishings have come through different adventures and discoveries in the back lands of post-Cold War Berlin; I have Sputnik ceiling lights and international clock faces from ex-Russian spy radio stations. There are original glass Bauhaus light switches and systems.

Tell me about your masks.
These are originals picked up or received here and there, and there are some of my early welding experiments. They are pretty eclectic in a collector's kind of way; a type of dislocation so as to conjure some past world.

Baby Mary

BOUTIQUE OWNER
STYLIST
TOKYO

LOCATION
HARAJUKU
WWW
bambifaline.com

I HAVE BEEN IN LOVE WITH TYPICALLY GIRLY THINGS FOR A LONG, LONG TIME

Baby Mary opened her boutique, Faline, in the Japanese city of Nagoya more than ten years ago. She launched a second branch in the heart of Tokyo after becoming a massive cult hit. The small space stocks Baby Mary's very personal, vibrant selection of fashion pieces, from labels including Marjan Pejoski, Jeremy Scott, John Galliano and Vivienne Westwood. Mary also works as a stylist for magazines and has party pages in style magazines commons&sense *and Dazed Japan. The cult fashionista splits her time between her homes in Nagoya and Tokyo. Her tiny apartment in the capital is walking distance from her shop, which is hidden down a side street, off the main drag of the fashion Mecca. Her home is very small, girly and full of pink. There is a lightness about the space, which opens on to a courtyard behind the brightly painted Design Festa art space. Although Baby Mary was initially deeply inspired by London, her home feels more Parisian, with photos of singer Uffie and books by Pierre and Gilles displayed around the flat. This is a space that champions the idea of girliness.*

How did the first Faline come about?
I was originally selling tableware and sweets. I was told that the building where I had my first shop was going to be destroyed. I grabbed the glasses, which I was selling, filled them up with tequila slammers and had a closing party. When they opened the new building in the same location the owners asked me to do something there again. I decided to start a new shop, specializing in Vivienne Westwood – who I was in love with. Faline was born! It grew into an edgy, selective shop that creates new fashion.

How did you end up coming to Tokyo?
I made a lot of friends through disco trips to London, Paris, New York and Ibiza. Then those friends around the world came to Tokyo. I ended up living here.

Then you set up Faline in Tokyo's Harajuku district?
Well, I joined Marjan Pejoski for a while, who was in Tokyo for three months to design stage costumes for a Japanese artist. During the stay I popped in to an estate agent's on a whim and found the space where Faline Tokyo is now. I instinctively thought, 'this is the place for me', but unfortunately found out it was taken already. This happened the day before my birthday and I had loads of champagne and tried to drown my troubles in drink. But all of sudden, Marjan called me and said that the sale could have been cancelled and to call the agency. Then I found out that it really was cancelled!

Do you do styling work as well as own your boutiques?
Yes. I have a regular page called 'Baby Mary loves xx' in *Dazed Japan* and I do styling work for *commons&sense* from time to time. I would love to do more styling.

How long have you been in your apartment?
Four years.

How did you find the space?
My estate agent called me, saying 'you'll like this space!'

What do you like about living in the heart of Harajuku?
It's cosy. We have everything here!

Tell me about how you decorated your apartment. Where did you get your furniture?
The wallpaper is left over from Faline Tokyo's fitting room. I have quite a lot of Cassina furniture. A lot of little things I found in Paris, Italy and Tokyo. Some are gifts and memories.

How does your home reflect your work?
I want Faline stores to be like my house.

Do you change your interior a lot?
I have to look after four shops and two houses, so I guess I will never be able to stop redecorating my spaces.

How do you think living in a small space influences what you do creatively?
Of course I prefer bigger houses! However, there isn't enough space in Harajuku. You have to live tidily. I used to be a slob but I had to become organized. Both Faline Tokyo and BABY FALINE (the one in Nagoya) are quite small, so maybe I'm good at making small spaces look good.

How does your home reflect your love of fashion?
Fashion is my life. I work at Faline as if I were working on my own home and I want to make the kids who come in to the shops feel like they are entering my own house. We welcome them with a cup of tea or go crazy with champagne. Hospitality is very important in all of my spaces.

Your space is so pink. Does that sense of femininity also reflect your boutique and styling work?
I have been in love with typically girly things for a long, long time. I always want to be sexy. I think my boutique is like a girl's bedroom. I used to dress up to look more avant-garde but now I'm girly. I'm very 'Lolita girl'. I can be the princess I always dreamed about when I was a small girl.

Page 15
Baby Mary
Pages 16 & 17
Pink bed surrounded by pink hats
and artwork
Page 17
Baby Mary's bedside table and books

Ludvine Billaud's creative talents are exceptionally broad. She studied textile design and graphic design and has worked in fashion and graphics in numerous guises from illustration to art direction. Her high-ceilinged home in Paris is open-plan but feels more decadent than loft-like. The apartment is essentially one room based around the kitchen and dining space near the street windows, and a bedroom and bathroom sectioned off towards the back behind wall partitions. The creative freedom of designing her apartment led Billaud to open her own café – Le Café Le Look. Part-coffee bar, part-gallery, the café is very much a space for collaboration and creative projects.

Ludvine Billaud

ILLUSTRATOR
ART DIRECTOR
CAFÉ OWNER

PARIS

LOCATION
STRASBOURG ST DENIS
WWW
ludivinebillaud.com

I CONSTRUCTED THE SPACE LIKE A PUZZLE

There is a real breadth to your work – art direction, textiles, illustration. What do you think holds your work together?
That's true. I mix many mediums. I get inspiration from all the fields I have studied. I never made a choice between textiles or graphics or fashion. Graphics is the only way I found to use all the tools I like. It is quite natural for me to think with different materials. For each project I try to find the cleverest answer. Sometimes I need to do an illustration, or cut out magazines, or design a typographic layout, or create a space sculpture.

What is the history of your apartment?
I moved here four years ago. I looked for a wild space to buy and found a big flat with offices. I split it into three parts with my brother. We destroyed everything first and separated the space.

Did you do anything to the space?
The first step was to destroy all the interior walls and to take off all the decorative stuff (mouldings, plinths, woodwork) from the window frames, the ceiling and the walls. I took the concrete off the wood floor. I wanted to reveal the basic structure of the space. After this big step, I analyzed the space. What I wanted was to create a break between wild old parts and new constructions. That's why it's not so Parisian in the end. The building is typical, but the space inside is more industrial or Belgian. That's the contrast I wanted. I also determined what I needed: a kitchen area, a bathroom, a bed area and the biggest empty space to organize a party or dinner around a big wooden table! I started to construct the space like a puzzle.

What do you like about the layout?
It's a unique space because there is no window at the back, so I was forced to keep the space open to drive the light to the back. That's why the bed area and bathroom are open. I also created a level under the bedroom to reduce the small effect of the space, and to create a dynamic perspective – and also to make a link with the entrance door, which is also higher. I like the contrast between the rough wooden floor and the geometric construction of the bedroom.

What attracts you to colour, in your work and home?
I love to play with colours. It probably comes from textile design, from my sensibility, from flowers. It's poetic and I trust the language of colour. For my home, I just told myself 'no white at all!', to contrast with all the white spaces people live in. I created a colour range with pieces of paper. I can be influenced by a graphic detail on a plate or a postcard or anything. I did not use dark colours. It's soft and pale, a bit 1950s. I also use

black (actually it's a very deep brown for walls and matt black for the floor) to contrast and make the other colours appear stronger.

Tell me about the drawings you created on the walls of the apartment.
The drawings you can see on the walls came from a shooting project I did with the photographer Cécile Bortoletti, for *HE* magazine (a Danish men's magazine). I started drawing on paper, but I finished drawing directly on the wall and I kept it.

Where do you get your furniture and objects?
I bought most of the objects and furniture from flea markets, especially in Burgundy and Brussels. I also bought a few items on eBay. I found the chairs in the street.

Tell me about your very unusual 1980s-style kitchen work surface.
I constructed the space like a puzzle and instead of building the kitchen along a wall I decided to show it like the main piece of the space. I designed the kitchen like a sculpture. My budget was really low, so the only option was to get an Ikea base. I spent a lot of time analyzing the catalogue and seeing how I could turn it

in another way! I first focused on the black shiny door surface, probably because it's the least 'Ikea'. For the top surface I discovered the old Italian Laminati print 'stratifié'. I found this 1980s-style raining grey-black motif. We built the kitchen in two days with a friend of mine who is a carpenter.

You've worked with a lot of fashion clients – Bernhard Willhelm, Cacharel, Kenzo. Does that inform your home in some way?
The graphic works I have designed for fashion designers are always specially developed for their own identity. For my apartment I was free, but the work process is similar and I can imagine it's easy to find links with my graphic works; it's the same sensibility, colours, a mix of materials.

Hardy Blechman

FOUNDER OF BRAND MAHARISHI

LONDON

LOCATION
WEST HAMPSTEAD

WWW
emaharishi.com

I'VE HEARD THAT A HIGHER CEILING WILL ALLOW YOU A GREATER FREEDOM OF THOUGHT

Hardy Blechman's label Maharishi is a cult brand that pioneered eco-fashion and streetwear. Blechman has constantly pushed the label – using experimental materials, working with fine artists, creating a plethora of camouflage-printed products. There is something magical about his Asian-infused house. The space is essentially one giant room, with a mezzanine bedroom at the top. Filled with dark wood, the calming space is filled with skylights and French doors that open on to a Japanese-style garden. It barely feels like London.

How did you start Maharishi?
I discovered hemp in the early 1990s and was really keen to promote that. At that time people were scared to do anything green, in case it ruined their business.

Does the label still have an Asian influence?
It's still called Maharishi. It still has lots of Eastern influences – the inspiration, some of the symbolism hidden in the clothing. One way or another, we explore the interaction between East and West. There are lots of things borrowed from Buddhist, as much as military, clothing.

You have created Maharishi pillows. Do you intend to do more interiors pieces?
We did a rug based on a Tibetan tiger rug. It's filled with US camouflage and flower-of-life patterns. We made speakers in camouflage with BMW. We did a championship backgammon set. The products are quite random. I'm yet to take Maharishi Home seriously – but it's likely that it will get my focus some time.

Tell me the story behind your house.
Very good friends of mine, Danny and Maggie, lived here in the early 1990s. I used to stay with them often and enjoyed my most formative, psychedelic experiences here. They were emigrating to Australia, and we had this crazy plan that we would buy some land together. They'd build a house in Australia, and I'd buy the house in London, and we'd switch between the two and share the houses. That didn't happen. Someone else we knew bought the place [photographer Glen Luchford], and about six or seven years later he was moving to New York. So we bought it. For way more money.

What is the story behind the remnants of wall mural?
The doors are French, I believe, from the 1920s. Glen put them in. Before, the wall extended all the way across. The place was originally used as a music studio, and then converted to an art studio. A lot of skylights were put in. Danny and Maggie had become friendly with the previous occupiers, who had been here for twenty years – Eddie and Sheila, who were a percussion musician and an artist. She worked on a piece for many years, directly on the largest wall. The painting was incredibly subtle, enormous and multi-dimensional. It was a crazy waterfall jungle scene. There are only remnants left around the edges.

What do you like about the openness of the layout?
I've heard that a higher ceiling will allow you a greater freedom of thought. That resonates with me. I lived in warehouses for a long time. I'm used to large spaces.

You have a lot of dark wood furniture.
Really it's a mishmash of things from the last twenty years. There's one large wooden Japanese table I found in Paris a few years ago. I like that kind of style. A lot of the wood is just bookcases I've bought over the years.

You have quite a dramatic Chinese chair.
My father was an antique dealer and I nabbed a few things from him. That was one of them. I think that's an early Empress Chinese chair design, which was heavily reproduced in the early twentieth century. Even now people make that chair, with dragonheads as the arms holding large pearls of wisdom. I always liked the symbolism of the dragon and the story of man taking a spiritual journey.

You own a lot of rare Michael Lau toys.
I have few pieces from Michael's cardboard series, which is probably my favourite. It was just around the time of the SARS epidemic in Hong Kong. When SARS came out, because people didn't want to go out, people were ordering vegetables and stuff online. Home-packaged box deliveries became crazily popular. It inspired Michael to develop this series of characters that look like cardboard and tape. Their hands have morphed into packing tape with serrated edges.

What attracted you to collecting Toby Ziegler's artwork?
I started collecting Toby Ziegler's paintings pretty early. Then I got involved in other ways. He started to experiment with reflective paint, but it didn't give him the result he wanted. So we worked together. I arranged a reflective fabric as a canvas, which he started to use around five years ago. His works are always about geometry and multiple perspective. So the reflective material added one more layer, where the perspective of light came in as well. I loved it and still continue to collect it.

Tell me about your interest in camouflage and swastikas.
I like symbolism in general. After some study and research, I found that camouflage was developed by artists, informed by the observations of natural historians, but it has been hijacked by the military. I wanted to make people understand that change. I think the example of the swastika is really relevant. It was a symbol that used to be positive. I was surprised to find that it was as widely used in Germany, England and America as it was in India, for hundreds of years. It seemed so shocking. If we could re-educate the public to understand the original value and discourage neo-Nazi groups from using it, we could shame them into understanding they are using a symbol that has a positive value for all people and no longer means Nazism. I think they'd have a lot less to fight with.

Gary Card

There is one word for Gary Card's work: wild. The young set designer has created some of the most memorable sets and props of the past five years – with editorial shoots for Another Man and Dazed & Confused, cardboard tribal pop costumes for fashion designer Cassette Playa, and a giant, wicker street installation. His home in Hackney is filled with sets left over from his work, some used as furniture, others spilling out of the corners of rooms. The flat is spread over three mezzanine floors, the central living space topped by Card's bedroom, with a sparse kitchen below. Card's own comic-infused drawings hang on the walls. Like Card's work, the space is brimming with objects and inspiration.

SET DESIGNER

LONDON

LOCATION
HACKNEY

WWW
clmuk.com

I THINK OF MY PLACE AS MORE OF A STORE CUPBOARD THAN A HOME

How did you start making sets?
I studied theatre design at Central Saint Martins, so I came from a set-design education. Although I loved the course and the subject itself, I knew I'd never make theatre professionally. When I graduated I became an illustrator for a few years, at the same time experimenting with small photo shoots, contributing bizarre props and headpieces. After a while the props became sets and the headpieces became costumes. It was a very organic process.

What appealed to you about working in fashion?
In the beginning I wasn't concerned with fashion so much. It was more about photography. I always wanted to make dramatic, exciting images, but didn't know what form they'd take. I remember seeing the cover Nick Knight and Alexander McQueen did for Bjork's Homogenic album when I was young, and thinking, 'that's the most beautiful thing I've ever seen! I want to make stuff like that.'

What attracts you to colour in your work?
When I first started making things I was terrible with colour. I wasn't confident enough to stick to a small palette; I just threw in every colour in the hope that the chaos would make some kind of sense. That just became a style I adopted. I'm a lot more discerning with my choices of colour now, but I still love using vibrant primaries.

Why did you choose to live in Hackney?
There's a great energy around here; everybody is making things. I love the people here, too. There's a great acceptance of weirdos around here – the impossibly cool, the mind-boggling eccentrics, the desperate try-hards, the tweedy young professionals. It's a great place for people-watching.

How do you think living in Hackney influences your work?
A lot my work is very collaborative. Most of the people I work with on a regular basis live in the area. I draw a lot of inspiration from my friends, too. We all help with each other's projects. It keeps you excited and motivated. There's a community feeling about it. I use a lot of found objects in my work, so I'm forever picking things up from the street and bringing them home, much to my boyfriend's disgust.

Tell me about some of the set pieces in your home.
I've thrown away a massive amount of work. It breaks my heart, but I have to in order to make room. I tend to hang on to stuff until I feel it's been properly shot, or if I think I can use it again. In my bedroom there are parts of a Santa's Grotto that I made for Comme Des Garçons' Christmas window and a costume set piece I made for Cassette Playa that we use as a kind of bedside table. Downstairs in the 'living room' there is a screen I made for a shoot for Another Man and some large props I made for my friend's music video. The kitchen is filled to the roof with about a grand's worth of foam cubes that I used in a story for a French mag called Mixed. I'm waiting for the right project to use them again. I can't bear to throw it all away!

How do you think your drawings connect to your set work?
For a long time I kept my illustration commissions and my set work very separate. My drawing was really a tool to illustrate the design ideas I was thinking about. Recently, however, they have both started to overlap. A lot of my sets are turning into huge canvases populated with paintings and drawings.

Tell me about your stuffed toys.
My boyfriend, Henderson, made them for his own pleasure. At the time he became quite obsessed with making them. He gave most of them away as gifts, but I insisted we keep a few.

What are your most strange and interesting things?
I think my Prince CD collection is my most interesting thing (I'm obsessed with him), but I'm sure most people would be bored to tears by it. I have loads of little Prince collections; Prince programmes, books, photos, magazine clippings, piles of bootlegs and singles. I'm afraid to say that I am a complete Prince geek… One strange thing that springs to mind is a floating ghost baby I made a few years ago. He's suspended from his umbilical cord.

How does the theatricality of your work fit into your domestic space?
That question suggests that I actually dress my place, when I really don't. I think of my place as more of a store cupboard than a home. I think the point is that it doesn't fit. It's at odds with the domestic space. It isn't easy sharing a flat with a lot of my work – it's large, clumsy stuff. Basically, it's a home for my work – it just graciously lets us stay here, too.

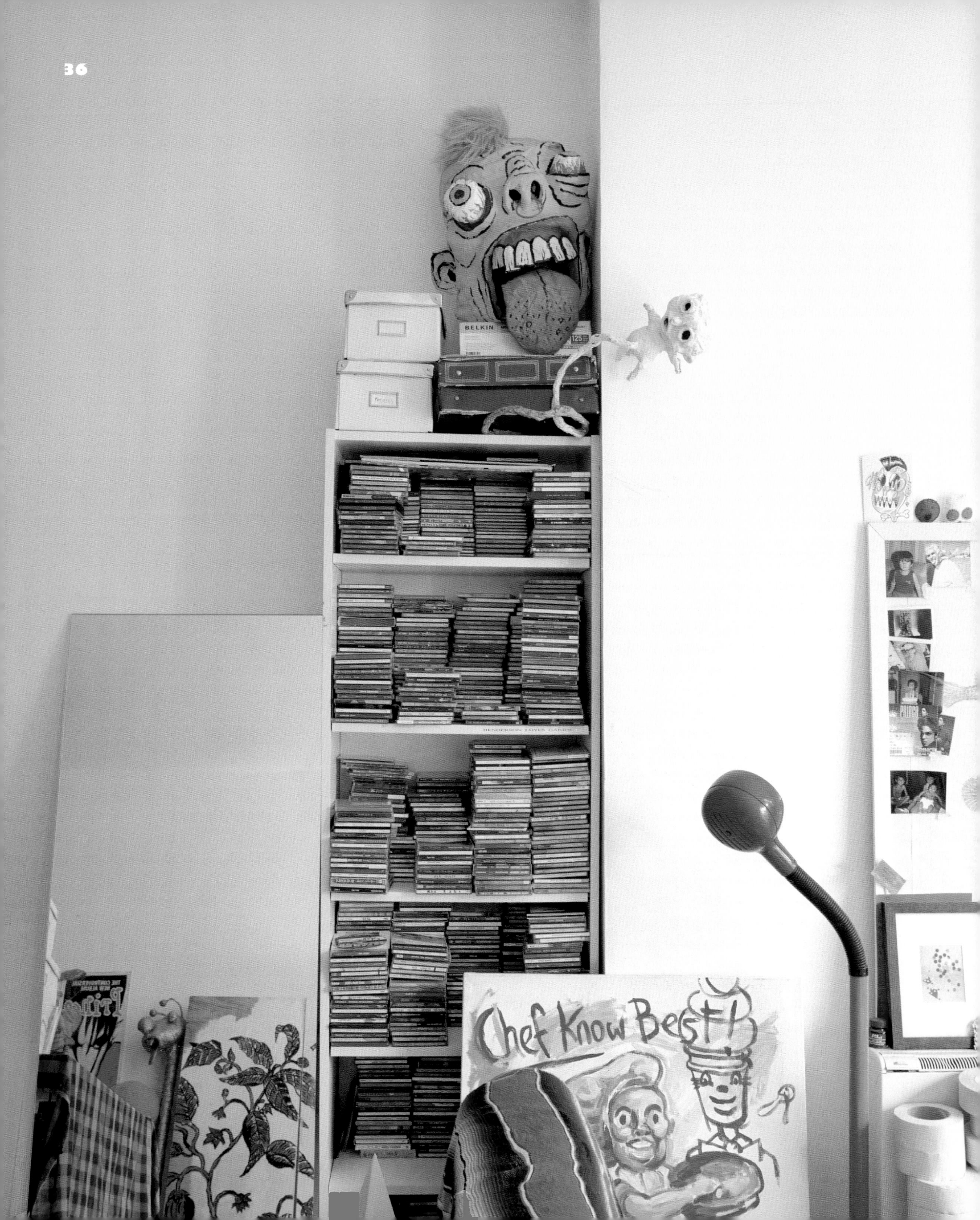
BELKIN
Chef Know Best!

Grace Cobb

STYLIST
CREATIVE DIRECTOR
LONDON

LOCATION
WESTBOURNE PARK

WWW
mapltd.com

I SUPPOSE NONE OF IT'S VERY WELL PUT TOGETHER, IT'S ALL A BIT BRIC-À-BRACY – HELD TOGETHER WITH SELLOTAPE

Stylist Grace Cobb's flat in West London is delightfully schizophrenic. Upstairs, there is an open white living space with graphic 1960s overtones, oversized signage letters and bright-coloured plastic storage. As you leave the space and enter the hall, things go from clean to chaos. Along the stairs is shelving covered in acres of weird objects, book and ephemera. The entrance to the flat is glowing black gloss. The space is like a three-dimensional scrapbook filled with odds and inspirational ends that reflect Grace's work as a fashion stylist and creative director of Wonderland magazine. Her home is the definition of eclectic.

How did you get started as a stylist?
By accident. I did fashion design at Saint Martins and didn't know what to do. I had a Saturday job and met someone there who knew someone who was a photographer. He said he needed someone who could get some clothes for him. I didn't know what that meant, or what a stylist was. That was twelve years ago. I started doing tests with him, and we got lots of stuff published.

Is your home an inspiration for your work?
Yes, but not directly. It's always subconscious. I collect old interiors books. I've got a David Hicks bathroom book and I'm slightly obsessed with that book. I love it. It's brilliant. But I'd never do my bathroom like any of those bathrooms. I just love to pore through it.

Is there a fashion influence in your home? The Pucci pillows, for example.
That's slightly embarrassing …They are stolen from Pucci shows. They are brilliant. Everyone was always so shifty about stealing them. You'd sit on them and people would stuff their coats with them. A friend of mine worked at Pucci for a while and she left with quite a lot of Pucci fabric. Enough to cover my chair downstairs. A very 1960s concept – get a Victorian chair and put a very modern fabric on it.

Do you think there's something British about what you do?
I suppose none of it's very well put together, it's all a bit bric-à-bracy – held together with sellotape. That's very British. Don't get too serious about it, because that's obviously embarrassing.

Although your flat has a white base, there's a lot of colour and objects.
Well, that's the crap that I collect, isn't it? That's the junk. I decided that because I do collect so much stuff, that I would do it in sections. So I could have clean space and then space that was full of crap, like all my trinkets and books and silly really tragic acres of crap. Living near a market I might as well drag the market home with me every Friday.

What are some of the things that you collect?
Crayon. It's a company from the 1960s and 70s that was sold in Habitat. I love it. It was produced by Airfix, weirdly. The colours are fantastic. They're just big containers. They come in all sorts of shapes and sizes and they are just genius. They're jolly and I love those primary colours. You can date them by the colours.

Tell me something about your large signage letters.
It's weird, isn't. It's just one of those things; I have no idea why I like lettering. I was brought up with a lot of lettering, because my dad was an art director, and he loved typefaces. If I see a nicely shaped letter, I love it. It's very pleasing.

Do you get stuff on your travels?
Yes, I do. I love going to hardware stores wherever I am, because you get such a good idea what a place is about by looking at hardware stores. I always get a bowl if I can.

What are the most unusual or strange things that you have on display?
I have some weird stuffed, but not real stuffed, animals. I sort of hate them now, but I can't get rid of them because they are part of the house. I think they are Victorian. They are little lions and tigers made of real lion and tiger fur. But they are not the actual size, and they aren't the actual stuffed animals. Their teeth are made from nails and things. They are really weird and primitive. I went to a museum in L.A., a really weird, tiny museum, and they had one of them – a black panther. In L.A., everything that is over about twenty years old is antique. It's probably not worthy of a museum – more like your granny's cabinet.

Tell me about the Edie Sedgwick wall print. It is so large it is almost abstract.
I did a shoot for Japanese *Vogue* a while ago – basically an Edie Sedgwick shoot. It was inspired by the film when she lives in a swimming pool, Ciao Manhattan. I nicked that poster from the set.

When you come in through the door it feels quite early 1970s, a bit cabaret.
I suppose that's because it's black and mirrored. The reason I painted the downstairs black is because there's no natural light in the hall. I thought, if there's no natural light then white always goes grey and cold. Why are you trying to get light somewhere that has no light? So I decided that the whole thing should be black gloss. It acts like a mirror. So if you put on a light and walk in there in a pink dress, the whole room goes pink. It's really exciting. It cocoons it. You don't know how small or big it is – you lose the edges. The poor blokes who come to read the meter think I'm going to chain them up somewhere and leave them for dead or something!

WARHOL

WARHOL MAKOS

magie

ANNIE LEIBOVITZ A Pho

BRUCE WEBER BLOOD SW
OR HOW I STOPPED WORR

arly Years of Fashion at Vogue

ANDY WARH
"GIANT

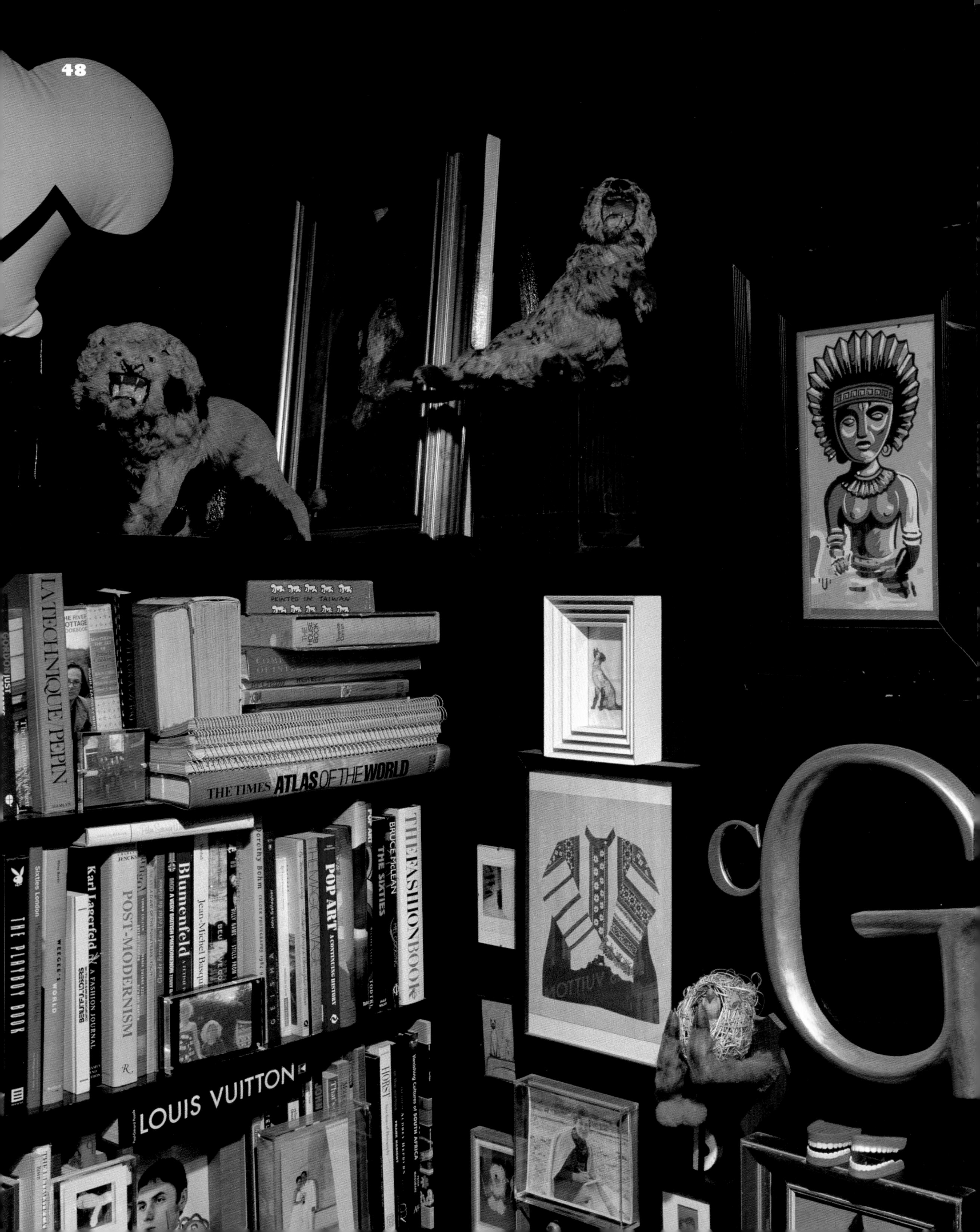

LA TECHNIQUE/PEPIN

PRINTED IN TAIWAN

THE TIMES ATLAS OF THE WORLD

POST-MODERNISM

THE PLAYBOY BOOK

Karl Lagerfeld

Blumenfeld

POP ART

THE FASHION BOOK

Jean-Michel Basquiat

LOUIS VUITTON

G

Yukinori Dehara

Yukinori Dehara's characters are intensely memorable. He creates handmade, twisted toys and sculptural figures from clay, which are transformed into vile and exceptionally funny plastic forms. Often there's a large dose of violence in his work. Bodies are severed, blood pours. Everything is exaggerated and grotesque, from anthropomorphic carrots to drooling pug dogs. He has created a number of pieces around yakuza, including the darkly brilliant animated TV series CAKEES, which was a perfect homage to 1960s Japanese cinema. Each episode focused on a different Japanese cake, which has the personality of a yakuza gangster. Dehara lives and works on the outskirts of Tokyo. He uses his domestic furniture, which he also exhibits in galleries internationally, to help make his characters. His home is a tiny space with traditional Japanese details that stand out against an ultra-modern, creative way of life.

How did you first start making figures and why?
I have enjoyed playing with clay since I was little – maybe three years old. In Japanese elementary school, we make dolls or a piggy bank out of clay. Making images in my head into three-dimensional objects, rather than two-dimensional drawings, is exciting simply because you get a feeling of the hands that created these objects. You get a different kind of pleasure than when you just draw with a brush.

Did you always want to make toys or did it grow out of illustration and drawing?
When I was a university student I was painting and designing. After graduation, I grabbed clay for fun and I enjoyed using it just like when I was a little kid. (At that time I thought that I should draw better or do something unique. I always had difficult thoughts in my mind when I was drawing.) I quite liked what I made out of clay. What hasn't changed since then is that I've always made what I wanted. Since I started making 3D works, I started calling them 'figures' since 'clay modelling' (nendo zaiku) in Japanese sounds like old men making traditional pieces. However, I'm not a moulding specialist who makes animation characters, so I came up with the title of 'figure illustrator'. Basically, I make only one copy of each figure, but I know that I can make mass-produced pieces that still reflect my style. So I also started making toys.

What attracts and interests you about bright colours?
I'm not that conscious when I am picking colours, but I naturally choose bright colours. It's been like that for a long time, since I was mainly drawing.

**FIGURE ILLUSTRATOR
TOYMAKER
ANIMATOR
TOKYO**

LOCATION
FUJIMIGAOKA
WWW
dehara.com

WHEN I'M WORKING, I STARE AT MY HANDS, SO IT'S IMPORTANT FOR ME TO HAVE A WIDE VIEW OF THE SKY FROM MY WINDOW SO I CAN REST MY EYES

Tell me about how you make your pieces. You use your living room table to bake them?
I draw a rough sketch – which is really simple, without colour. I make the figure with paper clay (the clay hardens very quickly, so I have about one hour for a figure). Not to break the pose, I fix the figure and let it dry naturally for one hour. When it solidifies a bit I put it on an electric stand and dry it some more – for half a day. I put the figure under a kotatsu (a traditional Japanese heated table) and finish drying it for two days. Then I colour the piece with acrylic paints. I decide the colour at this stage, which is my favourite part. Then I varnish it and the figure is finished!

How long have you lived in your apartment?
Eight months. I've lived around this Fujimigaoka station area for nine years. I have moved twice in that time so my address hasn't changed much.

What do you like about being in this more out-of-the-way part of Tokyo?
It's easy to get to cinemas and galleries. It's easy to visit the publishers and design companies that I work with. I am always looking at women riding on the trains. There are a lot of beautiful women in Tokyo.

Your work can be quite grotesque and delightfully disgusting. How does your home relate to what you create?
I'm actually not concerned about my home much. One desk is enough for me to work, so if I'm not too messy, it's OK. I don't decorate my space with cute stuff, but I put some of my works around for people to see. When I'm working, I stare at my hands, so it's important for me to have a wide view of the sky from my window so I can rest my eyes.

Do you think there is something specifically Japanese about the work you make?
I don't include Japanese-ness in my work intentionally, but I was born and live in Japan, so inevitably certain elements of Japanese culture come into my work. Manga, animation, toys, yakuza, zombies, porn, stress, Internet, TV, news, beer…

You have lots of art books and bright magazines. Do you research your work? Are you inspired by pop culture?
I love looking at art and illustration. I buy books or actual artworks when I can. They can serve as my idea source. But my space is quite small so I can't hang them all.

Aram Dikiciyan

PHOTOGRAPHER
TOKYO

LOCATION
AOYAMA
WWW
aramdikiciyan.com

SPENDING PRIVATE TIME WITH FRIENDS AT SOMEBODY'S HOME IS A VERY RARE AND PRECIOUS THING HERE IN TOKYO – PEOPLE TREAT THE PRIVATE PLACE OF OTHER PEOPLE WITH A LOT OF RESPECT

Berlin and Tokyo are an interesting combination. German photographer Aram Dikiciyan's traditional Japanese apartment in the rather posh Aoyama area of Tokyo manages to feel like both cities. There are traditional Japanese elements, like the antique table and the classic blinds opening onto a small terrace. Yet at the same time the space is filled with piles of books, magazines and artworks rising off the floor in studio-loft style. The space is largely monochrome – very much like Dikiciyan's photographs, which are often black and white. Somehow the apartment manages to feel full, but uncluttered; Zen-like, but not lacking in edge.

How did you become interested in photography?
My mom was a ballet dancer and my dad an all-round 'life' artist with a lot of passion and talent for drawing, music and languages. Music was always big in our family, especially classical music. My brother became a music engineer in Los Angeles. Of course I was influenced by this, but I didn't really find my passion for anything. I wanted to do many things but couldn't decide. I started photography quite late and by chance. Some friends started to publish a lifestyle and design magazine and asked me to do some photos. So I started photography more or less as a favour, with my dad's camera. I had never thought about photography before in my life. It was fun to see my first photos published, so I kept on doing some work for this magazine. I took very random photos of skateboarding, snowboarding and some portraits. Then I started fashion photography. That was the point where I started to see parts of my future, which made me want to study more about it. I kept on doing it until I decided to move to Tokyo to focus on a different life and a different photography. It took me a while, but finally I found my passion.

Do you feel your work has become more Japanese in some way?
Japan gives me a lot of influence and my life here, a lot of thoughts and creativity. Tokyo fills my heart with happiness and pain. A good mix.

You largely work in black and white. Why?
I try to show the shadow of life and love. For me, it's not possible to create that with colour.

How did you first find your home?
It was an accident. I tried to get an apartment down in Nakameguro, but all of a sudden my small, local real estate agent in Sangenjaya showed me this sheet with this beautiful, and for Tokyo huge and quite cheap, apartment in Aoyama. It is just a two-year contract because the house is too old and the plan was to knock it down after that time. I had visited some places to rent in Nakameguro that were very disappointing. It was easy for me to say yes to an even better area that was much more spacious for less money. For the moment I can stay here and that's great.

It's a very traditional space. Was that important to you?
I'm a big fan of Japanese lifestyle and traditions. It was easy to say yes to a place like this, but I didn't expect it. I like the tradition of taking off your shoes before entering. Spending private time with friends at somebody's home is a very rare and precious thing here in Tokyo – people treat the private place of other people with a lot of respect. The private place is the reflection of oneself.

What do you like about the monochrome simplicity of your home?
I need space for music and thoughts.

Tell me about your living room table.
It's an antique Ofen floor table. It's from Hokkaido, north of Japan, from about 1920. I just saw it and felt in love. It's heavy!

Most of your objects and books are on the floor rather than on shelves. What do you like about that?
Shelves would detract from the 'living on the ground/floor' atmosphere. The ceiling is quite low. The room becomes more spacious.

Where did you find the furniture and objects in your home?
In second- and tenth-hand shops, at Muji and of course at Ikea! There is also some stuff I brought from Berlin and on my travels.

Are you inspired by your space in some way?
It's a dream place for me and gives me a lot of positive energy. It makes me feel like I'm not living in Tokyo – but you step outside, and there it is. As an office, it's almost too comfortable.

GANZHEIT
aram
dikiciyan
PIPER
DIE WELT OHNE UNS
Das Ende ist mein Anfang
Daniel Kehlmann
PIPER
Französisch
Französisch
DUDEN
1
Die deutsche Rechtschreibung
Taschenwörterbuch Englisch
ILFORD
PANON
Paulo Coelho Der Alchimist
Paulo Coelho Der Zahir
Hermann Hesse Siddhartha
Hermann Hesse Demian
Franz Kafka Träume

Page 57
Aram Dikiciyan
Pages 58 & 59
The living room with Dikiciyan's work on the walls and projects and reference/reading material stacked on the floor

PARIS Fafi

I AM NOT ATTACHED TO THINGS – I LIKE WHAT I HAVE, BUT I COULD START FROM ZERO ANYTIME

Fafi's signature style is instantly recognizable. She creates sexy, curvy, pouting and exceptionally feminine girls. She began creating graffiti pieces in her native Toulouse in 1994. Her spray-can work developed into a graphic world, with characters that often reclaim female stereotypes. She has created toys, clothes, stationary, bags, make-up packaging, books, animations and, of course, paintings and prints – all emblazoned with her imagery. She lives in a bright open space in Paris with her husband, DJ Mehdi, and their child. Both Mehdi and Fafi work in the space, which they designed from scratch. There are skylights throughout the main level, and through the living room floor down onto the bedroom below. Brimming with colour, the apartment is a perfect reflection of the vibrancy of Fafi's art.

Your work has always focused on sexy, powerful girls. What do you like about those types of characters?
I've drawn girls – 'Fafinettes' – since 1994. It was natural for me, as a girl and a teenager. I was inspired by all my friends. I wanted to catch a kind of Polaroid image of the girls I knew – their attitude and style. Three years ago, I wanted to put more of me, my humour and my lifestyle into my work. So I came up with the Carmine Vault – the parallel world I've created. Inhabiting this world, we have the Fafinettes, of course, but also a bunch of other creatures such as Birtak, Hmilo and the Hillminis. They all live together, and have ways of behaving that suit this new world. It's a lifetime project that's just beginning.

How did you begin creating work in the street?
I was painting on roofs with a friend of mine. We were chilling up there and observing passers-by, who never looked up. We could paint and have fun without being seen. Usually, to get to the roof we had to climb several houses. It was a mix of stunts, magic and art.

Your work has appeared on so many objects. What do you like about that democratic approach to art?
I think it's cool to sell a canvas for $25,000 and a notebook at $10. I think it's nice if my young cousins can buy it if they want to.

How did you find the apartment? What appealed about it and the area?
We tried to get an apartment before this one. It was a commercial space, really amazing, but it was impossible to transform into something habitable. So I searched a long time for this space. I saw pictures of the place, knowing full well that it wasn't right for us because we needed more rooms. Anyway, we went here. It is on a one-way street with trees – very calm. I noticed that we could build another room within the structure of the building. We signed right away. The area's cool – between Père Lachaise, Bastille and République.

What did you do to the space?
We knocked everything down and rebuilt it. I spent four months on my moped, loaded with gear, spending all day with my team workers, designing everything. I made a few mistakes, because it was the first time I created a house and I had no idea about architecture. But I loved the process, and I can't wait to build the next one.

What do you like about living and working in the same place?
I am very lazy, so I need to make the least effort to go to my workspace. I just have to go up to one level, if I am in my bedroom, to draw or paint.

There's a lot of colour in your home. What attracts you to that?
I wasn't conscious of that. I don't think about things in general. I just do them.

Does your home reflect or inspire your work somehow?
Absolutely. Before living in this flat, we had another one. It was only one room. I had to build wooden platforms to paint on canvases. We just had our baby. I had to rethink the entire place in order to work. It wasn't easy and actually too restrictive to my work. Now that we are here, and each of us has our own space, we are more comfy with our own creation.

You live with DJ Mehdi. Does that music connection feed into what you do?
Yes, he always puts on music too loud.

What are some of your favourite objects in your apartment?
I am not attached to things – I like what I have, but I could start from zero anytime. Although I love the artwork I just bought by Amandine Urruty.

Where do you find your furniture? How do you make it your own style?
We have too many things from Habitat. It's disgusting, but I am forced to buy stuff from them, because they have things we are looking for. They create furniture needs we don't think about. I also have a dressing table and mirrors from my exhibition at Colette in 2006. I have always wanted one as a girly girl thing.

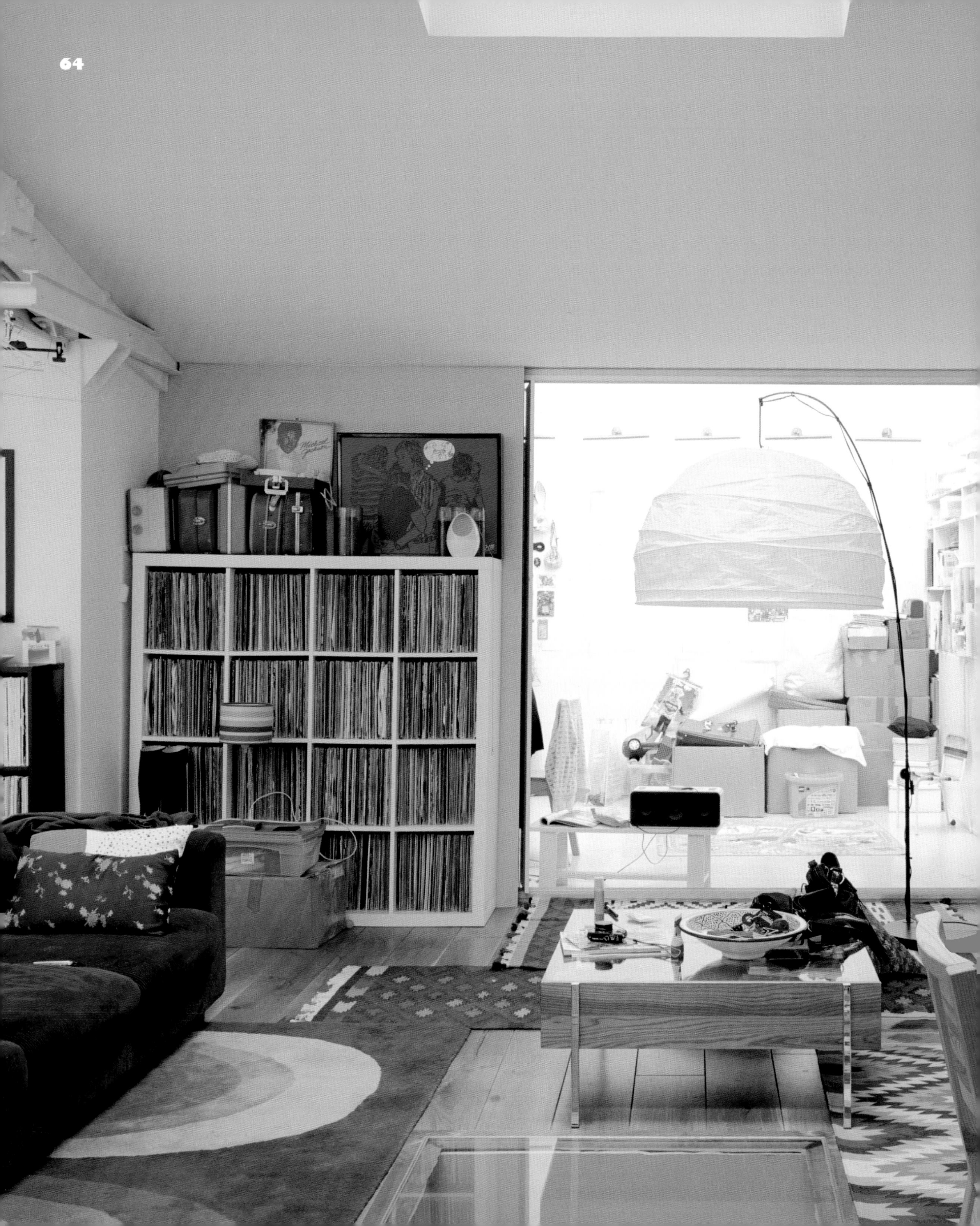
Michael Jackson

Page 61
Fafi
Page 62
Wall of Fafi's ground floor
studio space
Page 63
Fafi's ground floor studio space

Pages 64 and 65
The central living space looking onto
Fafi's studio
Page 65
The living space looking towards the
kitchen and mezzanine workspace of
husband DJ Mehdi

Lukas Feireiss

ARCHITECTURE
AUTHOR AND CRITIC

BERLIN

LOCATION
KREUZBERG
WWW
lukasfeireiss.com

MY HOME SURELY REFLECTS, IN ITS HYBRID COLLAGE OF THINGS, MY STATE OF MIND

Lukas Feireiss is not an architect. However, he knows more of the strange, creative, artistic end of architecture than most practising architects. His recent book SpaceCraft (2007) brought together the wilder end of architecture and art installation. His own home is arguably more liveable than the daring tree houses, makeshift installations and temporary structures he is fascinated by. His apartment, in the heart of Kreuzberg in East Berlin, is classically white with almost decadent details. There are walls of shelves crammed with books and almost religious displays of strange objects around the world. The vibrant, colourful details that fill his space seem more Mexican than East German. There is something organic and chaotic about Feireiss' approach to display.

How does Berlin inspire what you do?
I'm one hundred per cent Berliner. I was born and raised here, so I love this city, but I do need my distance from the city as well. I'd go crazy if I stuck around for a couple of months without leaving. It's a great place with lots of opportunities, a very comfortable nonchalant lifestyle with a lot of interesting and creative people. However, you've got to be aware of the fact that the city was built on former swampland. You can still sense that. People tend to sink here. Very boggish. Many people start out with promise and then slack away into constant partying.

What do you like about living in Kreuzberg?
I guess the most obvious characteristic of this part of town is its multi-ethnic and edgy mix of people. It's still pretty real around here; not as gentrified as, say, Mitte. It's more in your face. Even though times are changing here too. But up until now, I have experienced it as a real neighbourhood with a distinct, informal network.

How did you start writing?
While reading. The two go well together. I come from a classical humanistic background, so it was basic in my academic education. Having studied Comparative Religious Studies, Philosophy and Ethnology, I had to read and write all day. And if I have learned anything from all that, it's the insight that all is nothing but one big and beautiful wordplay. And I just love to play. Anyway, the few profound things in life that really matter remain silent.

You have quite a leftfield approach to architecture – the spaces in your book SpaceCraft, for example, can be very odd and unusual. Does that approach influence your own space?
It's fascinating to study the intense and diverse language of architecture and space. Growing up in an architecture gallery, the discussion and mediation of architecture played a vital role in my life from early age. Discussing architecture and space within the context of philosophy, literature and film has become a major driving force and inspiration for my own research and teaching. And just as I – as a non-architect – am interested in communicating architecture beyond its conventional disciplinary boundaries, I seek projects that express a shifting, multi-dimensional understanding of space. What I am looking for are spatial investigations that distinguish themselves through their poetic eccentricity and radical curiosity. Unique chances arise in the overthrow of the established etiquette.

How did you approach filling the space?
Return to zero. Throw everything out. Set basics in white. Fill with colour.

How does your home influence or reflect your work?
For me, a home is an emotionally charged expression of one's urge for originality in spatial structures. Our being strongly influences our consciousness and my home – in the broadest sense – surely reflects, in its hybrid collage of things, my state of mind. A constructive madness. My home is also my main base and retreat – and my overall source of inspiration.

There are lots of altar-like spaces in your home's interior. Is there a spiritual aspect to how you arrange stuff?
I call it Voodoo Kitsch. It's a collection of bizarre souvenirs and iconic keepsakes that I have found over the years and encompasses everything that matters to me, from Buddha to Jesus, from cowboys to samurais, from Godzilla to Wolverine, and from a boom box to a record player. Bizarre flotsam. Manifestations of beliefs and convictions. What particularly fascinates me about these relics and objects is the fact that they often represent a concrete, even if awkward, figuration of abstract and spiritual phenomena. It's funny how incredibly image-bound we are. We just can't cope with the ephemeral.

Do you have any unusual collections?
Yes, I do. I'm a collector. There's a collection of Buddhas from around the globe, ranging from a laid-back, fat-bellied monk to a slim-shaped, long-eared aristocrat.

Apart from that, I have quite a bizarre conglomerate of religious relics. Holy water, crosses, stones, sprays, voodoo dolls, Madonnas. I just love these queer little material manifestations of ephemeral ideas and beliefs. And last but not least, I have a great vinyl collection that covers everything from Mezz Mezzrow to the Ultramagnetic MCs, from Lee Scratch Perry to Fred Buscaglione.

Tell me about your shelves. How do your collections inspire what you do?
The wild mash-up of things very much reflects my rather unorthodox way of thinking and connecting seemingly unfitting topics. I take inspirations from everywhere. The farther away two things are from one another, the more I want to fuse them.

Although your flat is largely white, there's lots of colour. What do you like about that vibrancy and brightness?
I just like the contrast, the argument and the discussion. And I have never been too keen on accordance, anyway. White is the combination of all the colours of the visible light spectrum, and the great mother and child. All bright colours flourish and bloom against its background.

What are your strangest objects?
My all-time favourites are a spray can of holy air that I picked up in a market square in Mexico City; a little bottle of holy water from the Vatican; and a bar of soap from a little Indian store, depicting the archangel Michael, that cleanses you from evil spirits. You see, I am taken care of.

Nicola Formichetti

In under a decade, Nicola Formichetti swiftly moved from the shop floor of cult boutique Pineal Eye to become one of the world's most in-demand men's fashion stylists. Formichetti is currently creative director of Dazed & Confused and a senior editor of Another and Another Man magazines. He has worked as a stylist or consultant with a litany of major fashion labels, from Issey Miyake and Gareth Pugh to Uniqlo. The Italian–Japanese creative splits his time between his large warehouse space near Hoxton Square, New York and Tokyo, where he has his own store, Side By Side. His space is filled with artworks garnered from fashion shoots, including some memorable blown-up Mariano Vivanco photographs. Scattered among the retro furniture are Formichetti's soft toy collection, which spill onto surfaces with plush abandon.

How did you first become interested in fashion?
Both of my parents had a really strong interest in it, especially my mum, and it just rubbed off on me. Living in both Italy and Japan as a kid, I saw many different ways of wearing clothes, and going shopping with my mum was always exciting.

Do you have a specific look to your work as a stylist and creative director?
I think that I do have a strong idea of what I believe in. It's difficult to explain. My work is universal and encompasses different styles and cultures, whether I'm working on a specific image or a brand. Every job I do is different because as a stylist or consultant, your work is always a collaboration with a client or other creatives, who also have their own ideas on how their product or brand should be perceived.

What connections are there between your work and where you live?
I don't consider my work as work. Living, playing, working are all so closely tied together for me that the buzz of where I live has always suited my needs. I have been living in Shoreditch for ten years. It's where I feel comfortable, close to the Dazed office and all the photo studios. All my friends live close by. It feels more like a community than anywhere else to me.

How long have you been in the flat?
I've been living here for two years. My best friend used to live here. It was just a natural progression that when he moved out, I'd move in.

**FASHION DIRECTOR
STYLIST
LONDON**

LOCATION
SHOREDITCH
WWW
nicolaformichetti.com

I ALWAYS PICK UP TRINKETS AND LITTLE PIECES FROM AROUND THE WORLD, BUT IDEALLY I WANT MY FLAT TO BE A QUIET HAVEN

Tell me about your toy collection. How did it begin?
I've been collecting toys since I was a child. It's Japanese culture. They are everywhere! I don't have any specific toys that I like more than others, but I seem to have a lot of freaky-looking stuffed monsters.

Who are your artworks by, and how did you accumulate them?
I haven't bought any of them. I'd love to start buying art, but all of the artworks I have are gifts, or things left over after a shoot. The big yellow panels behind my TV are by Gary Card. I took them after a shoot we did together for Another Man magazine. Sølve Sundsbø has given me some prints of shoots we did together. Photographers and other people I have worked with have also given me pieces from projects they have worked on. I'm keeping them all so when the artists and photographers get really famous, I can sell them!

What do you like about having art resting against the floor?
I wish I could put them up on the wall. I'm sure it's not great for the artworks, but I just don't know how.

You have a lot of very large photographs from shoots. How did you come by them?
My dear friend Mariano Vivanco gave me these prints of a shoot that we did together for Dazed.

Tell me about your chandelier.
The chandelier was left over from my friend who used to live in the flat. I have just kept adding more and more jewels to it. I read somewhere that putting reflective things like mirrors and jewels to the north is good for the feng shui of a room.

Where do you get your furniture?
From dustbins to antique markets.

How does travelling influence your space?
I think it is evident from my apartment that I travel a lot. I always pick up trinkets and little pieces from around the world, but ideally I want my flat to be a quiet haven. I like it being minimal, but I can't help filling it with clutter.

Do you feel your home reflects your interest in fashion in some way?
I try to keep all of my clothing and fashion stuff in one room, so that on the rare occasions when I am not working, I can really switch off and rest.

Pages 78 & 79
Highlights of Formichetti's toy
collection

CALL ME CLASSIC, BUT I HATE TO SLEEP IN THE SAME ROOM WHERE I WORK OR WHERE I EAT

Spanish filmmaker Roger Gual's debut feature Smoking Room *manages to cover urban life, emotional stress, the changing definition of masculinity and racism. Quite a range for a film based around grabbing a cigarette on office breaks. Although there are touches of John Cassavetes and* The Office *in his approach, the results do have a specifically Barcelona edge – as does his home. Gual lives with his wife and two children in an apartment near the Barri Gòtic. The nineteenth-century building has authentic antique touches – traditional floor tiles, balconies and mouldings. But the interior is more modern, filled with cultural ephemera and split into different areas. Even if there are no walls in some rooms, one half feels mentally separated from the other.*

Roger Gual

How did you start making films?

Like all the good things in life, it just happened by chance. I was working in advertising in New York and Julio, a good Argentinean friend, was working in an American ad agency in Amsterdam. We both wanted to make a feature film – I had been studying film in Cuba – and he told me that he couldn't smoke in his office and always had to go out to smoke a fag in winter. And it was freezing. All his co-workers had ideas to try to do something against the regulations, but as soon as they got back into their offices, they completely forgot about all the complaining. I thought this was a great start for a film based in Spain, where everybody was used to smoking everywhere. So we shared some thoughts and started to write *Smoking Room* – our first feature film.

It took two years to finish the script. We both moved back to Barcelona and tried to get financing from TV stations and government money, but everybody said no. We convinced a bunch of good actors to do it for free and share the incomes if some day we had them. We finally shot in five weeks with no money and a DV camera. After six months' editing we had a pretty good film nobody could watch. So we decided to take it to film festivals. We won three big prizes at one of the biggest festivals in Spain; one for the script, one for the actors, and the special jury prize. Since then the film has opened in theatres and had a really good response. Once, in a taxi, the cab driver said to me he really liked my film. From that moment, I knew I wanted to make more.

Barcelona seems almost to be a character in your work. What interests you about the city?

I think my work is really influenced by Barcelona, but the stories I try to tell could happen anywhere in what we call the 'occidental world'. It's funny you mention it, but not a single recognizable image from Barcelona has appeared in any of my films. The most important thing when you are making a film is reaching universal feelings; it doesn't really matter where it's been shot.

How long have you lived in your home?

I moved into my flat when I got back from NYC ten years ago. I knew I wanted a big flat, since in NYC you are forced to live in one-bedroom flats – sometimes even without a kitchen. It's an 1865 building, first built for rich families in the nineteenth century who had servants and everything. But during the 1950s the whole building became a textile factory, and most of

the flats were used as storage spaces. I moved in 1998 with my girlfriend and we had to build a new kitchen and bathroom to make it liveable. We had this massive roof party as a house-warming – so nobody could spoil the newly painted walls in our flat.

What do you like about the space?

I like it because it's an open space without being a loft. Call me classic, but I hate to sleep in the same room where I work or where I eat. It has eight balconies facing the street, so there's lots of natural light and that's good if you live in sunny Barcelona. The area is very close to the city centre, so we cycle almost everywhere.

How did you decorate it?

It's a mixture of expensive design furniture, things we bought in flea markets and on trips we've made, and Ikea stuff. My wife is an interior decorator, so that helps.

Although it is largely open-plan, you strongly differentiate between areas. Why is that important?

As I said before, I like to cook and eat in the kitchen; read, work and watch films in the living room, and sleep in the sleeping room. I hate those flats where you have to take a shower in the middle of the living room, because the interior designer thought it was funny.

How does your home influence and reflect your work?

I think the flat reflects my personality and my cultural background. But I could be writing the most amazing love story from the worst place on earth and I bet you couldn't tell the difference. All I need to write is my laptop, my iPod and a plug. I work from home most of the time.

What are your favourite items in your home and why?

My Eames chair and my ottoman are where I feel most comfortable to work. They are the first things I'd save in a fire. Right before my wife and two kids.

Page 81
Roger Gual
Pages 82 & 83
Gual's lounge area
Page 83
The book and music corner

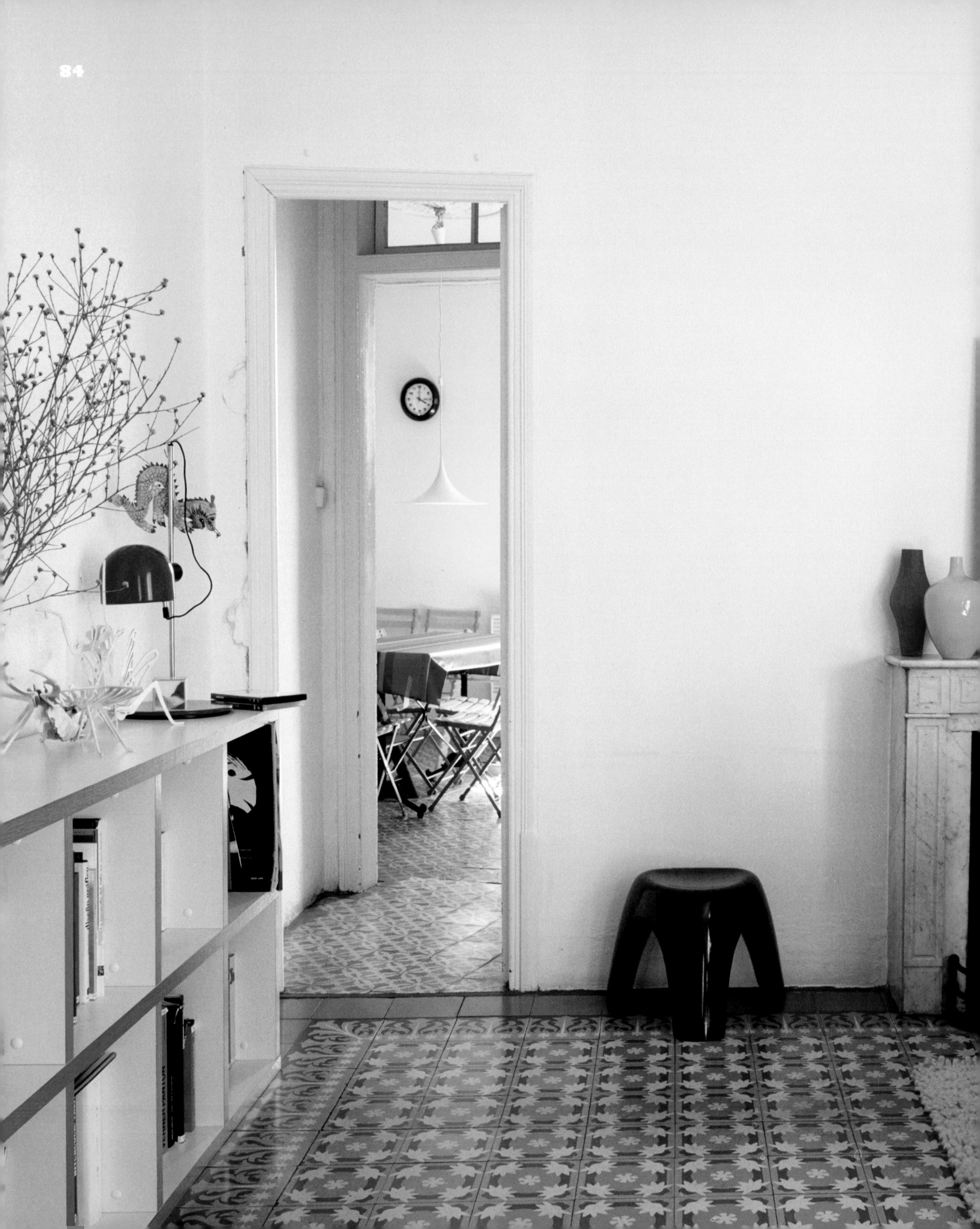

Pages 84 & 85
View from the book corner into
the kitchen
Page 85
Gual's workspace

Jaybo, a.k.a Monk

**ARTIST
ART DIRECTOR**
BERLIN

LOCATION
KREUZBERG
WWW
myspace.com/jayboakamonk

I WILL ALWAYS CHANGE MY STYLE; FOR ME THAT'S AN IMPORTANT SIGN OF EVOLUTION IN WHATEVER I AM DOING

Jaybo has turned his talent to everything from art direction, graffiti, graphic design and his own streetwear label. In recent years, the self-taught artist has become best known for founding German magazine Style and the Family Tunes and for a body of violent, urban pop artworks, which reference everything from Francis Bacon to Mickey Mouse. His pieces range from giant street murals to paper cut-outs to stylized comic-influenced acrylics on wood. His home, in a quiet southern part of Berlin, is a bright space with windows overlooking a park. Each windowsill has a small collection of found, often natural, objects. The furniture has a retro edge – worn brown leather or late modernist wooden tables. Jaybo's paintings line the walls alongside pieces by artists like Barry McGee. The space, where Jaybo often works, is full – but in a peaceful, quiet way.

How did you end up in Berlin?
I came to Berlin around 1984 or maybe 1985. A beautiful love story brought me here. I fell in love with a Berlin girl. I met her in Toulouse (south of France) and she decided to show me the place where she used to live. After two weeks in Berlin I lost my passport. I could not get another one so easily, the Wall was still up, so I had to stay.

Did you start as a designer or an artist?
I left school when I was 14, so I don't have any diploma or school structure of any kind. I jumped from little jobs to doing my own business, working at bars, normal stuff. But I always drew from when I was a child, until now. I never stopped. On the other hand, I never wanted to be a designer or an artist, I just fell into it. In 1994, I founded the clothing label Iriedaily with four other freaks. None of us knew how to sew any clothes. We just did it, and over the years we learnt how to fall. We made mistakes and then we learn not to make that mistake again. A simple recipe.

How would you describe your approach to art?
Art is quite a new thing to me and I guess it will take a long time before I can understand what it really means. I learnt to always express my feelings visually – call it art if you want, but for me this is just a normal part of my life. All I am able to feel, good or bad, will be transcribed into a picture, a piece, an object. I just do it. I do art like I play music – first a monotone melody, then the rhythm, then a hook.

Your visual style seems to have changed a lot over time. How has it developed for you?
I will always change my style; for me that's an important sign of evolution in whatever I am doing. Movement is the only way to have stability or harmony. Fixed things are dead. So I will always try to find new dimensions, asking myself new questions, finding new problems and solutions. I don't ask myself much about what has changed or not. I try to live in the present moment. I think that the future is made from fears and the past from regrets – so that doesn't leave me so much choice.

Tell me about being art director of Style *magazine.*
Well, *Style* is a monthly magazine, so I am busy with it every month. I feel like it's my kid. The older I get, the less it needs me. I have a wonderful team around me, and it's fun to see the magazine growing, changing, trying new things. I love it.

You have so many creative outlets – design, fashion, art. How does it all fit together for you?
It's tough. It was easier before, but now I need one day or two to recover between jobs. I am very good at focusing. When I do one thing, I won't think of the others. I am 300% into the job I do.

Do you work at home?
Sometimes, but I think home is made for my family, and for chilling.

How long have you been in your flat?
Nine years, almost ten years now.

What inspires you about the apartment?
The view. This is the only place I know in Berlin where you don't see any kind of buildings. I just see trees. I am above the trees and I got the simple privilege of a natural horizon, which is essential for my recovery time.

You have a lot of retro 1960s furniture. What appeals about it?
I don't know. Maybe the fact that I was born in the sixties. I love that period's naive way of believing that we could leave for the moon tomorrow.

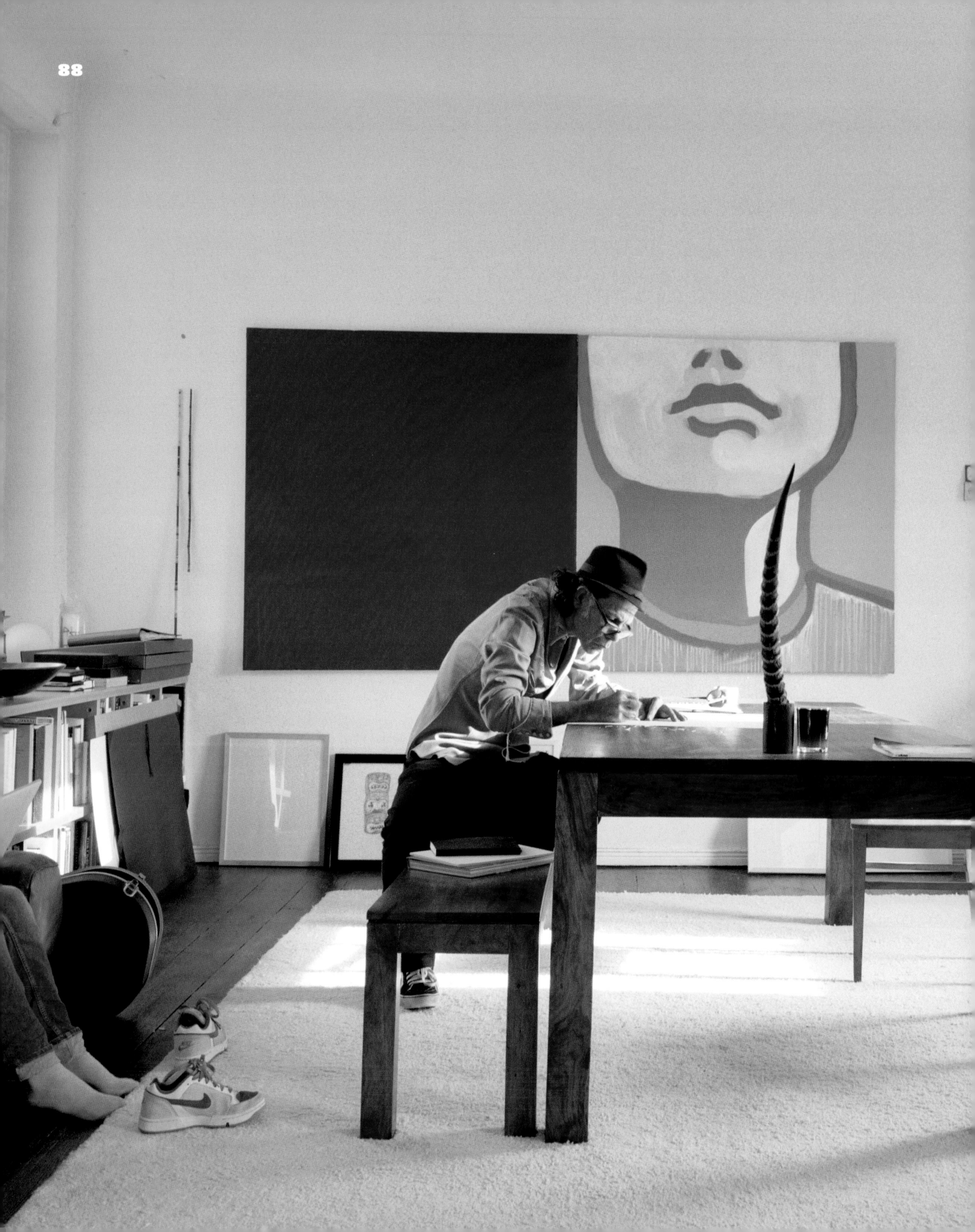

Page 87
Jaybo, a.k.a. Monk
Pages 88 & 89
Jaybo at work at living room table
Page 89
Work in progress

Pages 90 & 91
The corner of the living room under
the stairs leading to the bedrooms
Page 91
A selection of Jaybo's early artworks

Johann Haehling von Lanzenauer

The aristocratically named Berliner Johann Haehling von Lanzenauer has worked as a creative consultant and creative director for companies like Nike, Levis, Nokia, contemporary art museums and magazines for a decade. He is also a well-respected art curator, now with his own gallery space in the Mitte area of the city. Lanzenauer has championed shows by leftfield artists like Shepard Fairy, Beautiful Losers' curator Aaron Rose, Geoff McFetridge, Steve Powers (Espo), David Lachapelle and Ben Sansbury. His interior strongly reflects his taste in contemporary art. It's a cut and paste space where the walls display a changing selection of art, where classic Victorian details and white space sit next to street artworks and scrapbook walls.

How did you start Circleculture?
We started Circleculture in 2001 with my business partner Dirk Staudinger. The idea was to create an innovative hub for design and creative research and to establish a cultural platform in Berlin for the global urban arts community. So we were able to rent this gallery space in the centre of Berlin and an office in Hamburg. From there we had this art space called Circleculture Gallery where we showed artists, which back then, where total underdogs in the established art world. The kind of street artists, which today are sold in the auctions next to Warhols and Basquiats.

When did you move into your home? What appealed about it?
I moved in the summer 2007. An East German doctor used to live in this space for over 40 years. It was totally trashed out and had this typical East German smell. I fell immediately in love with this ancient atmosphere, the large rooms, the whole history breathing through those walls. Also I liked the fucked up brown-grey walls outside which reminds me how most East Berlin houses looked like when I moved to Berlin 15 years ago. Today most houses are rebuilt and almost clinically clean. They lost their soul. The other thing appealing so much is the skate park in the city park directly in front of my dining room. I always dreamt to have a skate park in my garden. Now I'm almost there.

**CREATIVE DIRECTOR
CURATOR**

BERLIN

LOCATION
FRIEDRICHSHAIN
WWW
circleculture.com

I LIKE THE ECLECTIC APPROACH – IT MAKES ROOMS MORE ALIVE, CREATIVE, COMFORTABLE, SOULFUL, INTERESTING

Do you think there's a relationship between your gallery and your home?
Yes it could be seen as a kind of extension to the gallery. There's a constant exchange of pieces by Circleculture artists we hang. Often we have dinners with artists, curators, museum people, collectors and other friends at my house. When they come from outside Berlin they stay in my guest room.

Tell me about what art you own. What are your most unusual pieces?
There's a piece by Dash Snow I love. It's a very simple photograph of Dan Colen in a shadow. I bought this piece at Contemporary Fine Art Gallery during his Berlin show last year. Then in the hallway you'll find many pieces and photos, which somewhere have an autobiographical context. Each piece stands for a part of my life. Works and pieces by Ed Templeton, Anton Unai, André, Minor Threat, Shepard Fairy, Peter Sutherland, Taro Hirano....And then of course the framed Beautiful Losers silk screen series.

Tell me about the ladder piece in your dining room.
The rope ladder is an installation by artist Anton Unai. The ladder leads into a black hole which is just a black spot in the ceiling made out of colour. With the ladder as a symbol for escapism, the fake hole refers to the fact that always trying to escape never will be a solution to solve fears and problems.

Your bedroom, in contrast, is really white but manages not to feel minimal. What did you like about that whiteness?
My bedroom is the place for coming down. Here I can empty my thoughts.

You've got an interesting contrast between new and old - industrial lights in the hallway next to — vintage heating. Is it an intentional contrast?
I like the eclectic approach — it makes rooms more alive, creative, comfortable, soulful, interesting. The pure and straight design approach is more something for museums, galleries or shops where the presented items need place to breathe and to develop their qualities. My home is more a place for living, laughing and loving and less a sales or presentation room.

How does what you do reflect on how you decorate your home?
As I'm pretty much involved in urban fine art, street art and design culture, of course, many things come home. I collect pieces from artists, curators, musicians and designers I meet in my life. Recently I found three different artworks on cardboard from the same artist in different streets of Berlin. I don't even know his name. Now those huge pieces will be hung in my guest room. I'm so happy about them!

Tell me about the image wall in the kitchen — what's on it? How did it develop?
It started from the 'I love Berlin' sticker in the classical 'I love NY' aesthetics. From there I started to put photos and pieces close to my very personal Berlin. My daughter, friends and colleagues. Also you'll find a prayer book of a Buddhist sect with a sticker by Shepard Fairy on top saying: 'blind acceptance can be hazardous'.

Idris Khan & Annie Morris

ARTISTS

LONDON

LOCATION
ISLINGTON

WWW
allsoppcontemporary.com
victoria-miro.com

WE LIKE THE WAY THAT THE HOME CAN FEEL LIKE AN ART INSTALLATION

Idris Khan and Annie Morris provide a perfect example of how to compromise two very different artistic approaches in one home. Khan creates large-scale photographs, layering appropriated images into haunting works that question authorship. Morris, in contrast, creates paintings and sculptural pieces that are more rough, hand-finished, and full of colour. Their modern flat in Islington, which is full of art, is a refreshing combination of old and new, chaotic and clean — but always creative.

How did you start making art?
Annie: When I was around eleven years old, I remember having no sustained concentration on anything except for art. I would stay up all night painting. The compulsion to paint and draw was the way I understood art. From then on I knew I wanted to be an artist and I sold my first painting that year – a painting on a wooden box.
Idris: I was a late starter. I started taking art seriously from the age of 18, when I found the perfect medium to express my ideas – photography. For me art came after sport, messing about in a poor art class, and being surrounded by no culture in a small town just outside of Birmingham. My art became a type of search into a culture I never had.

How do you fit together your different approaches to art in your home?
Annie: My art is about the accumulation of materials, of bringing found objects such as broken wood, metal, reused canvases and painted clothes pegs together. Although random, I make them fit. I have always collected antiques and strange objects. I hardly ever throw things away.
Idris: I think the place would have much more junk everywhere if we didn't live together. I have a much more minimal and clinical approach to making art, which I guess I try to bring into the home. I like clean lines and Danish furniture. The combination of the colourful objects that Annie accumulates brings quite a unique style to a room. I don't think I knew what colour was until I met Annie – now I see it everywhere.

How long have you lived in the space?
Idris: I first moved here when I was a student at the Royal College of Art in 2003. Annie moved in November 2007. It wasn't a home before that.

Where do you get your furniture?
Annie: My family home was a huge influence. I love my mother's taste and wherever we went in the world she dragged me to tons of antique markets where I was forced to look at endless French monogram linens! I have ended up stealing so much stuff from her. The last thing we bought was an old ladder from a junk shop on Holloway Road. I painted it five times to get the right colour to fit the room – there is something wonderful about making something your own.
Idris: The main light in the home was bought from a Danish furniture store, as was the Eames chair. But the bigger pieces – the dining table, wardrobe and writing desk – were bought at auction.

There are a lot of different kinds of chairs in your space.
Idris: We like the mixture of old and new. Mismatching chairs around a table seems to add charm and character to a room. We were inspired by Jacques Tati films – his playful use of placing a lot of different chairs within a room. They become very sculptural, and apart from everything it is inviting to have many chairs in a room.

Apart from your own work, tell me about what else you have on your walls.
We have a work by Giuseppe Penone, who teaches at the Beaux Arts. A lithograph by Maira Kalman. We have a naive painting from the 1960s done in bright colours, a Rob Ryan cut-out, a Peter Doig print, a Tal R, a David Shrigley drawing, a pair of glow-in-the-dark Chris Ofili works, a group of Madge Gill postcards and a huge book piece by an artist called Etienne Rotzaffy, who only paints on books. Everything else was made by us.

Annie, you lived in Paris for a number of years. How did that influence your interior?
I lived there for over five years, in a gorgeous flat just near the École des Beaux Arts, where I studied. I often went to the Montreuil and Clignancourt markets. What I admired about the French interiors that I saw was the way that rooms can look totally unexpected, but still be so sophisticated and smart. There is a casualness, where everything just somehow finds itself in the perfect spot.

Tell me about some of the stranger objects on display.
We have a wire chicken that has become a fruit bowl, five large beaded animals handmade by an African outsider artist and a pair of beautiful pots painted with black ink breasts that we bought in Cuba. An antique Donald Duck teapot, a ceramic red crab ashtray and clothes pegs – lots and lots of clothes pegs!

There's a lot of pattern in your space – floral pillows, graphic artworks, mixed colours. What attracts you to that?
It makes a space feel richer. We like the way that the home can feel like an art installation. Different colours of an object are repeated throughout the room, like it's one piece. It's nice to be surrounded by beautiful things, whether it be objects or work by an artist who inspires us. We just choose things we love.

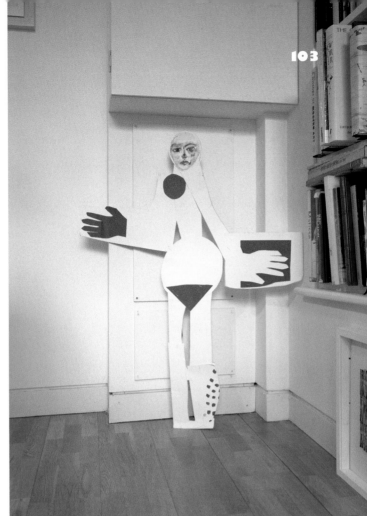

Wes Lang

ARTIST
NEW YORK

LOCATION
BROOKLYN
WWW
galleriloyal.com

I WANT TO LIVE IN THE COUNTRY IN A CABIN SOMEDAY — THIS IS THE CLOSEST I COULD FIND IN BROOKLYN

What do you get when you stick a wood cabin in the heart of urban New York? Something close to artist Wes Lang's Brooklyn apartment. The living space, towards Greenpoint, has cabin-like wood-panelled walls and is filled with taxidermy, skull ephemera and exceptionally odd discarded objects. Lang's own artworks pepper his room — drawings of American Indians on ageing brown paper, fascinating fusions of erotic bodies and skeletons, a mirror emblazoned with the black outline of a naked girl. The apartment, like Lang's work, plays with America's historical heritage and darker undercurrents. Just as Lang scavenges strange imagery to incorporate into his paintings and drawings, so his home is an outsider museum of forgotten things.

How did you find the apartment?
It was originally my brother's apartment. He was moving in with his girlfriend (now his wife) and I was breaking up with the girl I was living with at the time. Perfect timing.

What's the home's background?
We don't know too much about it, but apparently several people have died in it. My roommate, Ernest Loesser, used to work with a girl whose family lived here. She told him it was haunted. Every once in a while there are pools of water in strange places in the apartment… Very strange.

Tell me about the wood walls.
I wish I could take credit for them, but it came this way. They are made of beautiful old knotty pine. I want to live in a cabin in the country someday – this is the closest I could find in Brooklyn, until I can get out of here.

Did the walls inspire you to fill the room a certain way or reflect the taste you already had?
The walls definitely reflect a taste I've always had. It is filled with relics I have been collecting for years. I'm attracted to things from the past. This home is the perfect backdrop.

Would you agree that your place somehow feels like travelling back in time?
For sure. Every time someone comes over they comment 'This is what my grandma's house looked like' or 'I feel like I'm out in the woods'. It has a wonderful smell of wood and cigarettes, like an old bar, and I love old bars.

There are a lot of dead things in your space, from skull imagery to dead animals. Why do they appeal to you?
Ever since I was a kid I have collected skulls. My skin is covered in them, my walls, my work; I'm just obsessed. I certainly have a strong fascination with death.

What taxidermy do you have? Where did you get it?
I have a lot. A white cobra fighting a mongoose found in Stockholm. A pheasant my mom gave me years ago as a present. A piranha my sister-in-law got me for Christmas. For some reason I get a ton of dead animals as presents. My favourite is the deer butt monster. I got it off eBay. The guy described it as 'perfect to put in your cooler after hunting. Tell your wife to open it and look what you killed on your trip. Scare the hell out of her.' Amazing.

Where do you find your objects?
Everywhere. Like I said, many are things I have had since I was a little kid. I'm just a collector by nature. Books, records, tattoos, motorcycles and just strange shit that makes me smile. I grew up in a house filled with these kinds of objects, so I guess I have no choice but to carry on the family tradition. I spend tons of time at flea markets and have a terrible eBay problem.

How does your place reflect your art?
Well, I have several of my favourite pieces I've made hanging in it. My drawings and paintings reflect an America from a long time ago. This apartment certainly makes me feel like I'm living far in the past. I'm actually working on a project right now that will be a big cabin, and all the artworks will be hanging inside of it instead of the gallery walls.

Are you inspired by where you live?
For sure. It keeps me in the right headspace. I spend my first few hours every day just sitting in here thinking, before I can go out and face the world. It calms me down before walking out into the shitstorm of New York.

You've got sentences scribbled on the walls and ceilings. How did they happen?
It started on a drunken night with my friend Brian Montuori. Most of them are song lyrics. My favourite is 'I'll bring the fuck you's'. That pretty much sums up a lot of me. It says 'my dreams are beyond control' on the kitchen wall. That's from the Bob Dylan song 'Dear Landlord'.

What are the strangest things in your room?
I really like my Oddfellow banners. Beautiful hand-stitched images of death and rebirth. The deer butt monster is way high on the list. It creeps people out. I stare at it all the time. I have a tattoo needle made in Burma in the late 1800s. That's a pretty good one. The tramp art furniture I have is pretty great too. The stuff is made out of old cigar and fruit boxes. My grandfather's shotgun is in the corner. That's my favourite for sure.

Your own work hangs in your room — but from really different periods in your life. Why do you choose to live with it? How do you feel about the pieces you keep?
They are all pieces that mean something special to me. There are only a few things I make that I won't sell. These are the works in my house. Each of them reflects a milestone in my 'career'.

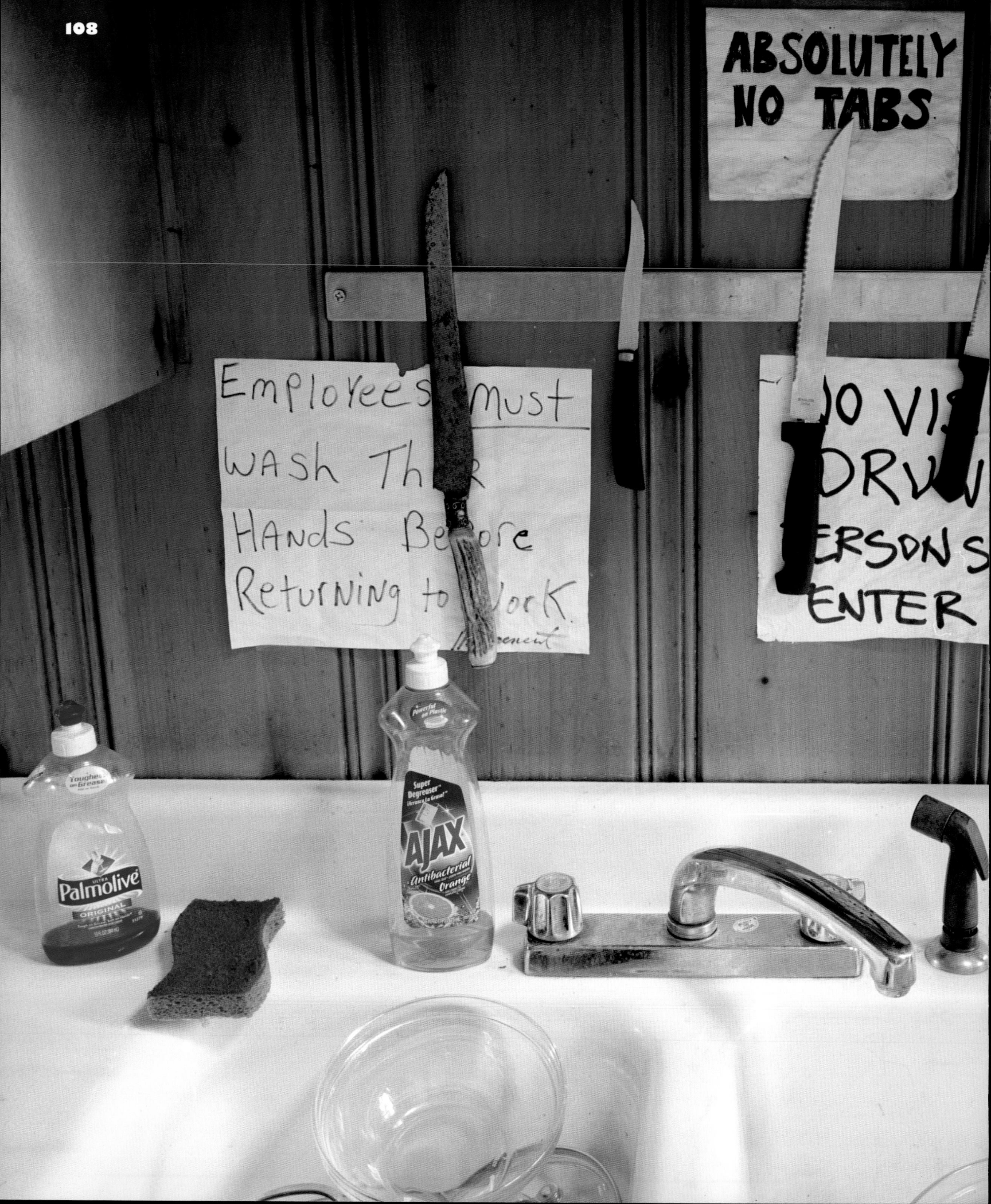

ABSOLUTELY
NO TABS

Employees must
wash Th r
Hands Be ore
Returning to ork.

O VI
RV
ERSON S
ENTER

Palmolive
ORIGINAL

AJAX
Antibacterial
Orange

109

Page 105
Wes Lang
Pages 106 & 107
Views of spaces either side of the
windows in Lang's living area
Pages 108 & 109
The kitchen sink
Page 109 (top & bottom)
Some of Lang's collection of objects

My dreams are beyond control.

Pages 110 & 111
View from the bed onto living area
Page 111
Wall texts

Artus de Lavilléon

ARTIST

PARIS

LOCATION
MARAIS
WWW
artposthume.com

IF WE LIVE IN A ROOM, ART IS THE ROOM, AND THAT IS WHAT MAKES IT SO BEAUTIFUL

Artist Artus Boutaud de Lavilléon has had a varied creative career. The Parisian auteur has owned a gallery, created cult zines, drawn illustrations for style magazines including Jalouse, worked on a collaborative art project with iconic fashion designer Jean Charles de Castalbajac, and exhibited his own drawings, paintings and installations. His tiny but fascinating one-room flat in the Marais reflects that multiplicity of creative projects. De Lavilléon works at a desk beneath his bed surrounded by his own work. Scrawled texts on found paintings hang alongside autobiographical, monochrome drawings. The crammed room is a reflection of Artus' changing fascinations and the intensity of his approach to art.

How did you start creating art and illustrations?
My mother encouraged me to draw a lot, paint, play music, run in the woods, see the beauty of this or that, and, mainly, to look. When I was around six, my stepfather drew a perfect white circle on a wall inside of our house. I was fascinated. I think that was my first artistic emotion. Later, I discovered the work of Malevich, and that my mother used to be one of Guy Debord's best friends. I was skateboarding a lot and had this strong connection with the streets.

How would you describe your approach to drawing?
When I was 20 or so I really wanted to be a cartoonist, but I ended up in an art school were everyone made fun of my 'Mickey's'. It was the 1990s and everyone was really into contemporary art. I just hated it, but I discovered painting. Being an 'artist' was more of an adventure. Around 2005, after I was involved in different projects (a skate magazine, two shops, a gallery), and I had the crazy life I wanted (sleeping in the window of 'Le Printemps' for 15 days, writing an art manifesto, doing the Gumball Rally), I felt really tired and escaped in the countryside. I started drawing again. I would take a picture, copy it, and write whatever came into my mind on it, mainly personal stuff. I did 12 copies of the original fanzine *Deadpan*. I just found the perfect tool to express my life, my doubts and expectations. It was satirical, funny, sad and human.

There is something very emotional and personal about a lot of your work.
I am a human being, like anyone else, and I want people to feel with me – and to feel with them. I am not sure that my things are more real than an abstract painting… but maybe it is easier to relate to it. I can't stand contemporary art because it makes you feel so small when you don't understand it and so powerful when you can buy it. It seems so cold to me.

Tell me about your flat in the Marais. What is its history?
The flat belonged to my father, and it is a typical 'Chambre de célibataire' (bachelor pad). It's a one-bedroom flat on the third floor of an old building. I moved here in 1994 with my future ex-wife, two years after the death of my father (after a huge fight with my stepmother for it). For two years we lived in this tiny 15-metre-square room without even a shower. I think she ran away when she realized that this room was not only my room, but also the centre of my life. Later on, my mother moved in. She was an old depressed drunk unable to take care of herself and even walk. I took care of her, found her a flat three stairs below, and helped her to get her life together. There are a lot of stories about this flat. I love it as much as I hate it, but it is still my base and it is good to have one.

How has your interior developed?
For ten years I collected lots of things, until it was hardly possible to breathe. I had eight huge bookshelves crowded with things, including one in the middle of the space. My bed was stacked in between this and that, and my artwork was on top of everything. After a decade, I exhibited my room in a gallery and put it on sale. The idea was to give an opportunity to someone to buy a part of my life: my books, files, tapes, clothes and everything that was in the room. Unfortunately, I haven't sold it, but I still have great expectations for this project. The testimony of a period of life, probably what art posthume is all about.

After my show, I ended up with an empty room; I didn't even have a bed… I met an amazing woman, Eleonora, and we fell in love. Together we built a new environment for the both of us. A mezzanine, several libraries, and a closet. The idea was to have Eleonora's side, and my side. Hers would be quite empty, very clean and white, near the window, with her couture equipment, and mine messier, as it always is with all of my art stuff. We even have a shower now.

How does the space influence the kind of work you create?
I don't really care about the lack of space, but it is true that it influences my work a lot. I wish I could work on a bigger format on a daily basis, but it is okay. It pushes me to think more about what is really important for me to say through my work. 'Art is an environment in itself and a feeling, art is life. It gives form to the space that separates us.' If we live in a room, art is the room, and that is what makes it so beautiful.

Page 113
Artus de Lavilléon with his girlfriend
Eleonora
Page 114
De Lavilléon's artworks, shelving and
fridge door
Page 115
The workspace beneath the studio
bed
Pages 116 & 117
The studio seen from the front door
Page 117
The front door and Artus' artwork

Ryan McGinness

Ryan McGinness is an artist whose work fits as easily into the pages of Artforum as it would inside a skate magazine. His layered baroque paintings brim with curling graphic shapes and calligraphic lettering. There is something stylized about his approach. It is not surprising that he worked at the cult graphic design company Pentagram in the 1990s. His artwork explores the visual language of branding and his images are often filled with overlapping logos for imaginary brands that seem to simulate the experience of the visual overload of modern life. He has collaborated with Agnès B, shown at Deitch Projects, as well as cult shops Colette in Paris and Alife in New York. His pieces have been snapped up by NYC's MoMA and by Charles Saatchi in London.

McGinness' apartment in New York is calm and an interesting contrast to his kaleidoscopic paintings. The overall effect of the one-bedroom space is white and bright with unexpected touches. The living room is filled with green foliage and houseplants alongside a blood-red velvet ornate sofa and a 1960s pod chair. Pieces by Faile and KAWS hang over rococo-style candelabras. Many of the walls of the apartment are covered in giant blown-up photographs with a touch of idyllic kitschness – a Swiss landscape or an acre of long grass.

How did you start making art?
My interest in art was encouraged at a very young age. In grade school I attended the Old Donation School for the Gifted and Talented in Virginia Beach and continued my studies there through high school. I then attended Carnegie Mellon University in Pittsburgh, where I studied art and design. After graduation, I moved to Manhattan, where I have lived and worked ever since.

Your work originally reflected graphic design in some way, but you really pushed against that in your paintings. How do you think your work has developed?
Graphic design is a service industry, not an aesthetic. I am not interested in design, but I am interested in form. I learned how to develop iconic forms through a drawing process that has historically been employed by the design industry. However, my goal is to use the visual language of corporate identities and public signage to communicate something personal. I want to use a universal language to reflect local thoughts.

How long have you lived in New York, and how does the city influence your approach and work?
I have been in New York since 1994. Yes, the aggressive pace at which this city moves influences the way I work.

How did you find your apartment?
I was looking for an apartment that was within walking distance of my studio. My apartment is in the Meatpacking District and my studio is in Chinatown. It's a brisk half-hour walk, which can provide me with a healthy break when I have time.

Why did you create the walls covered in blown-up photographs?
I used photo-mural wallpaper of a mountain in my foyer and a bamboo forest in my bedroom. I just thought it would be funny. I found them online.

Where did you find the stained-glass door to your bedroom?
It's an interesting contrast to the modern space. I found the door at a great shop in Harlem called Demolition Depot.

Tell me about your furniture – a lot of it veers from plush decadent velvet to cool simple whites. What do you like about that contrast?
Contrasts are inherently interesting because they are about clash and conflict. If you can make those conflicts harmonious, then you've got something even more interesting. My last apartment was very cold and uniformly modern with a lot of expensive finishes. It was consequently not very comfortable. With this apartment, I was trying to make something a little more fun.

There are lots of plants in your apartment. What do you like about that?
I like the organized chaos of the plants. They are all in the same matching pots, but, of course, all do their own thing.

Do you think that the emphasis on foliage and nature in your work relates to the natural forms in your home? Are you inspired by your space?
Yes, definitely. I am not influenced by my space; rather, my space is influenced by my work.

What do you like about candelabras?
The candelabras are symbols and placeholders for fanciness. I make an effort to hunt for them in flea markets wherever I travel.

Tell me about the artworks you own.
I have a Faile work on paper, the two KAWS prints from 1997, a painting by Daniel Trochio, a print by Tim Ayres, a photograph by Matt Clark, and a work on paper by Will Cotton. I have other pieces in my personal collection, but my place is too small to hang them. The other pieces are stored in my studio.

What else influences and inspires you?
I like metaphysics and comedy.

ARTIST
NEW YORK

LOCATION
MEATPACKING DISTRICT
WWW
ryanmcginness.com

CONTRASTS ARE INHERENTLY INTERESTING BECAUSE THEY ARE ABOUT CLASH AND CONFLICT

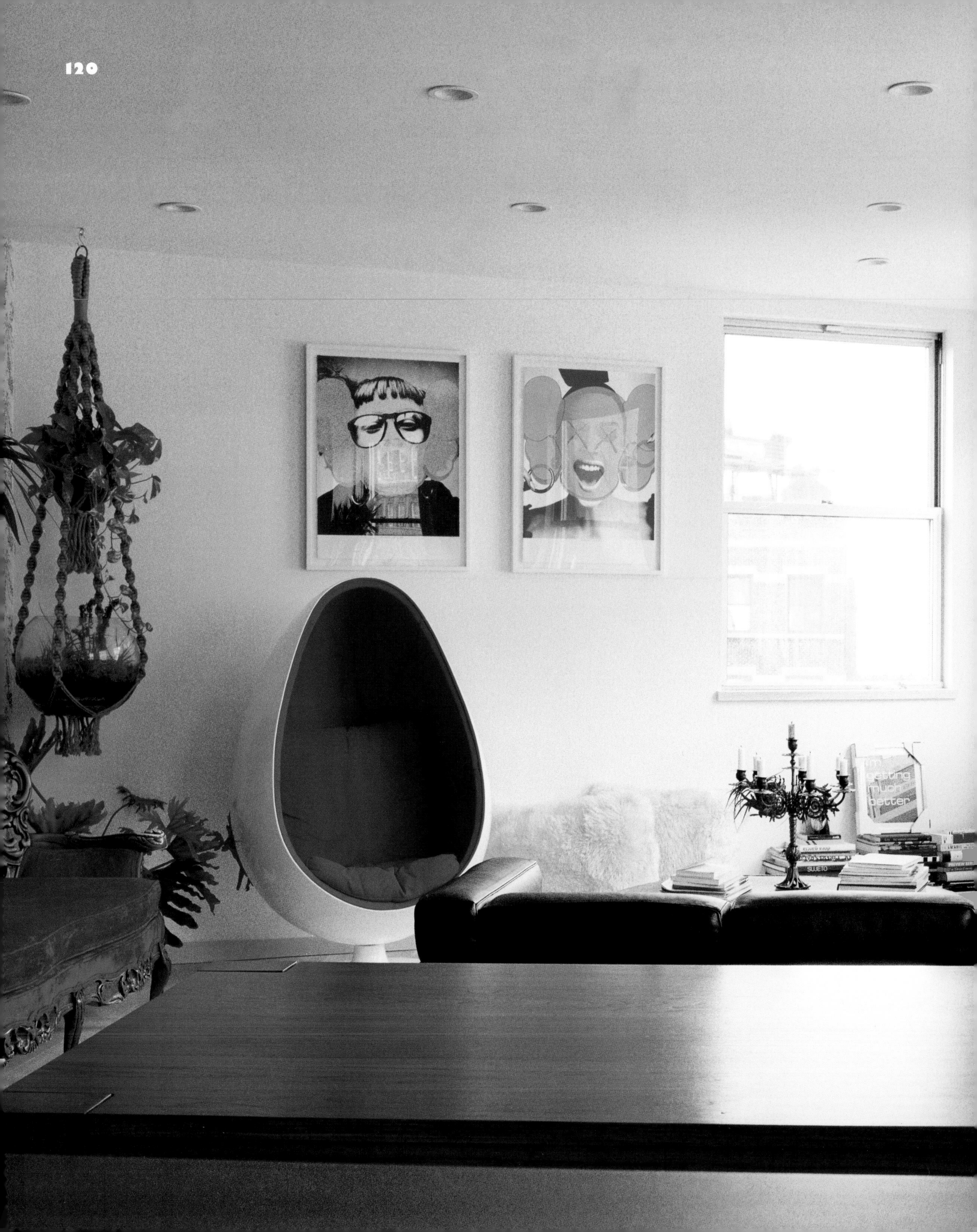
i'm
getting
much
better

Page 119
Ryan McGinness
Pages 120 & 121
View of McGinness' living room
Page 121
View from the living/dining area into
the bedroom

Pages 122 & 123
McGinness' bedside reading matter
Page 123
Detail of corner of living room

Leah McSweeney & Rob Cristofaro

FOUNDER OF FASHION LABEL MARRIED TO THE MOB; CO-FOUNDER OF CREATIVE STORE, GALLERY AND BRAND ALIFE

NEW YORK

LOCATION
TRIBECA

WWW
marriedtothemobnyc.com
alifenyc.com

THE APARTMENT HAS BECOME A LOOSE INTERPRETATION OF WHO WE ARE AS PEOPLE

Leah McSweeney and Rob Cristofaro have both created some of the best-known and most inventive streetwear brands of recent years. Alife was one of the first shops to sell pop collectables alongside street clothing – redefining how design ephemera reflects a way of life. Married to the MOB was one of the first female-only street brands. The pair live with their daughter, Kier McSweeney-Cristofaro, in a spacious loft in downtown Manhattan, which is also the office for Leah's company. Although filled with wood and natural materials, contemporary pop culture details do still sneak into the space – from monkey art toys to graffiti-influenced paintings. The space is a creative take on the idea of something homely and comfortable.

How did you start Married to the MOB? What was the idea behind your approach?
Leah: MOB pretty much started after drinking some white wine on my stoop and talking shit with friends. All the guys had T-shirt lines, and seemed to be making somewhat of a living off of it. There were other lines out there that made men's and women's stuff, but no line that was for females only and that really represented the female gender. I wanted to make a line that girls would be proud to rock. I knew MOB had to embody my past, present and future, my life, my likes and dislikes, and basically what it takes to be a Most Official Bitch.

And Rob, what was the idea behind Alife?
Rob: Alife was the combination of a creative studio/retail space/gallery and workshop, all under one roof. The aim of Alife was to create a space that embodied the lifestyle of its creators. It was to be a place that people would come to, to experience new things in old New York.

Does your store Alife Rivington Club influence your interior in anyway?
Rob: The Alife Rivington Club influence came from the old-school tailor shops of London. The interior of the apartment is pretty much as raw as it can get for an old NYC loft space. Exposed beams, exposed brick and floors; if you look through the cracks, you can see your neighbours.

Tell me about the objects on your shelves.
Rob: Honestly, the past year has been a big adjustment period for Leah and myself. We had the baby, moved into this place, set up a home office… I think the apartment has become a loose interpretation of who we are as people. I usually have many more objects on display; things that I have collected along the way.

Why did you put the swing indoors?
Leah: My dream has always been to live in a big-ass loft. Growing up in a small, modest NYC apartment, I am milking all the space, and just kind of showing off with the swing. I told Rob that I was buying a swing off eBay. I think he thought I was a little crazy, but he loves it now.

How did you end up in your space?
Leah: When we found out that we were expecting our daughter, Rob and I realized that our old place on Spring Street just wasn't going to cut it. It was too small and had too many annoying drunken people at night throwing up on our stoop. Plus I wanted to move my office into the apartment, so I could be with the baby as well as continue to grow MOB. There are very few true lofts left in New York and we found one! We did build two walls to make two rooms. We really wanted to leave it completely open, but I knew it was important to have a separate space for the office.

Tell me about the artworks you own.
Leah: The photo above the dining room table is by Henning Bock. He is a German photographer whose work we found in a gallery in SoHo. The photo is of a scene at the Museum of Natural History. The Fuck Em painting is an original piece by Craig Costello (a.k.a. KR of Krink fame). I love curse words! We curse all the time. Everyone in the garment and retail business does. At first we didn't think we could hang the piece up – because of the baby. But then we realized she's probably going to be aware of these words anyway… We just have to teach her not to say them.

What's the story with the lips?
Leah: I've always loved lips. They are classic, pop-art objects. I also use lips in my MOB logo. It's like having a big piece of MOB in our living space.

There's a lot of wood in your home. New York is such a concrete city. What did you like about that material?
Leah: We love the country and the outdoors. We are actually building a house in the Catskills. I am planning on using as few pieces of wood furniture as possible. The loft reminds me of a hunting lodge sometimes, so we will be doing the opposite in the Catskills house.

How do you think your work is influenced and inspired by New York City?
Rob: Our work is NYC. We are NYC. We both were born here and grew up here, so the work is a direct reflection of New York Shit.

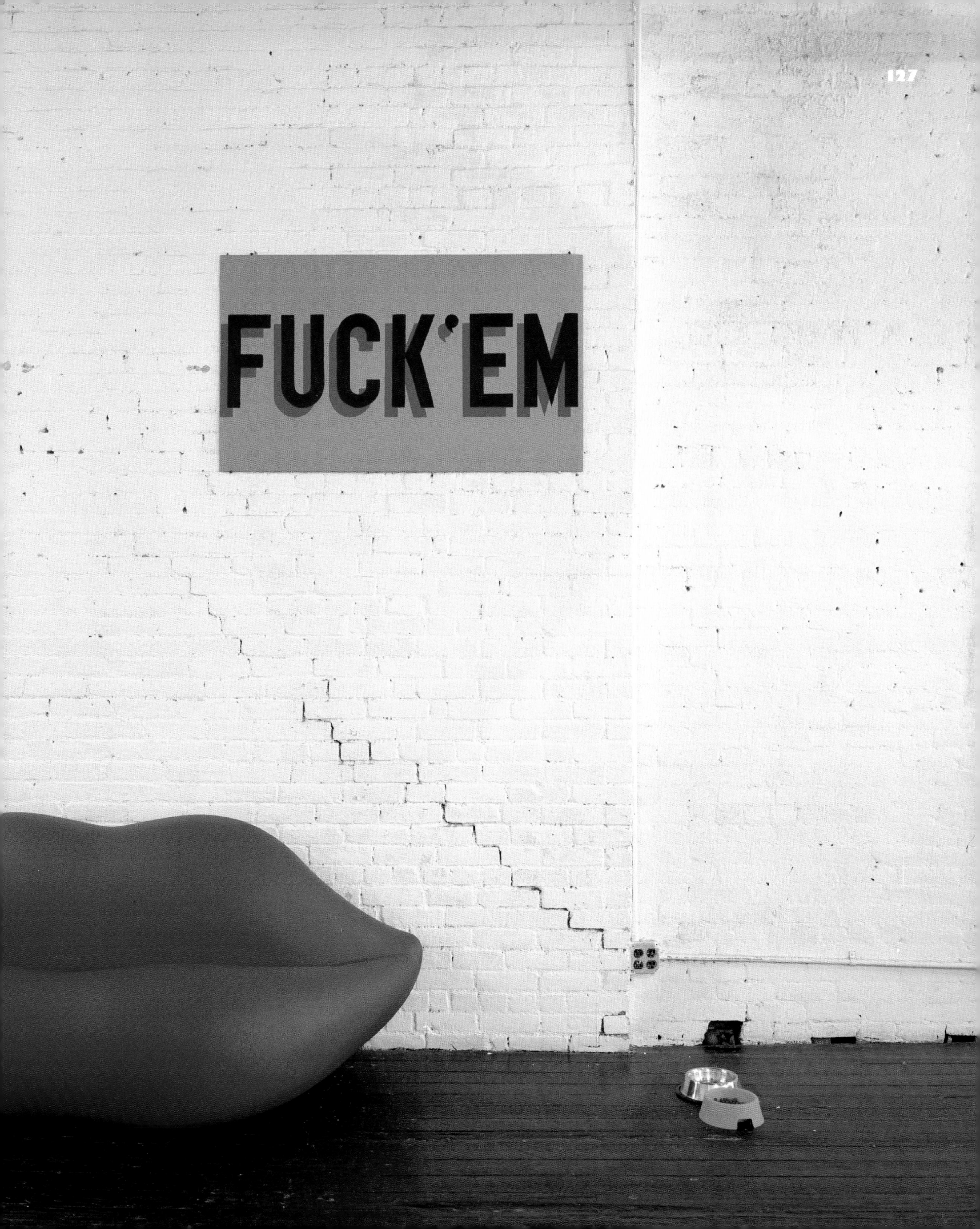
FUCK'EM

Van Neistat

ARTIST
FILMMAKER
HALF OF THE NEISTAT
BROTHERS
NEW YORK

LOCATION
MANHATTAN
WWW
neistat.com

WHEN YOU MAKE THINGS FOR YOURSELF, THERE'S NO MANDATE BESIDES YOUR OWN STANDARDS

Van Neistat really likes DIY. His enthusiasm for electrical wiring, hardware stores and DIY catalogues is evident everywhere in his New York apartment. The bed is a mattress laid on three-wheeled trucks. The specially designed lighting is all exposed wires and multiple switches. The dining table is rough handmade wood. The artist and filmmaker's compact apartment also has notable creative additions – the credits from Buffalo 66 are painted above the kitchen. The bathroom walls are plastered with 1980s cheap posters from shooting ranges. The window blind is a map of the world. The result is a home that is refreshingly leftfield – very much like the art Neistat creates.

Have you always made work with your brother Casey?
No. We started out independently making shorts. Casey lived in a trailer in Connecticut. I lived in NYC. After he moved here, we began our collaboration. I like working closely with my brother. I like that I get to see him nearly every day. Also we have very similar points of view as we are from the same place. Casey is brilliant, and takes pleasure in things I hate to do. Also, he's a terrific artist.

A lot of your artwork seems intentionally provocative. What do you like about making art that pushes people's buttons?
When you make things for yourself, there's no mandate besides your own standards. If you can make things that look or smell or taste or sound nice, then people will ingest them. So you can show people your ideas that normally would have no venue, provided you can make your ideas pretty.

Why did you decide to create most of the furniture in your apartment yourself?
Because my apartment is so small any furniture had to be custom-made in order to fit properly. I like that whatever I make is made exactly how I like it, and I like the gratification of a job well done.

Tell me about the process of filling your space.
My wife and I picked out the apartment. Then we rented a van and drove to Toronto. This was back when the American dollar was stronger than the Canadian dollar. We went to an amazing modern furniture store on Queen Street right near Lake Ontario and bought

some furniture we liked, including a stainless steel garbage can that deli-bags fit into perfectly, and smuggled it across the border. We placed the furniture where it belonged, then built things as we needed them. A brilliant designer named Fiona Jack once told me that lighting was everything, so I designed some lighting on paper and then built it.

Where did you find the furniture you didn't make?
That place on Queen Street in Toronto. The couch we found on Craig's List. I'm actually not that crazy about it. The desk chair I bought at the D and J thrift shop in Orange, Virginia.

What attracted you to those kinds of retro pieces?
I think Europeans and Americans build the best stuff. And our best manufacturing days are behind us, at least in the US. So to find the really nice stuff, you sort of have to go back in time.

You seem to be obsessed with electrics. When did you first become interested in them?
When I worked for [the artist] Tom Sachs, he gave me a bunch of electrical projects to build. So I got the skills from him. We made a miniature McDonald's that actually worked. Then I just started messing around with it.

How do you think your apartment reflects your work?
I made everything in my apartment the same way I make things for work. Our studio in Tribeca has a lot of the same motifs as the apartment.

Why did you paint the Buffalo 66 credits on the wall?
I forced my wife to paint that. I really love the movie, and I love the look of the credits. I love the '66' title. It takes up the entire frame!

Tell me about the Daniel Johnston video sculpture.
Daniel Johnston is an artist who makes music the way we make movies. He's like an unintentional genius. He made this song called 'Speeding Motorcycle'. This radio station asked him to perform it with a band in the radio studio, so at the moment of the scheduled performance, he called in and sang it over the phone while the band played live in the studio. The sculpture is the lyrics written out with a Dymo label maker, along with the scrap paper of the lyrics that I wrote the Dymo labels from. The song in the video is 'Speeding Motorcycle'. The video in the video is the lyrics popping

out of the label maker. The Dymo sort of sings along. I made it for my wife for her birthday. We got married on a motorcycle trip, and we both ride.

There are other motorcycle pieces around the apartment. What do you like about having bike objects in your home?
I dressed up as Evil Knievel on the Halloween before he died, so I just left the costume, which was hand-painted on a chef's uniform, on a hanger on a hook on my closet door. I like the colours. The helmet lamp is a memento mori that tells me 'be careful'. Tom found the helmet on FDR Drive. Motorcycles are a huge part of my life.

Page 131
Van Neistat
Page 132
Exposed wiring above the
bed made by Neistat
Page 133
View towards the kitchen
and front door
Page 134
Vintage furniture near the
apartment's windows
Page 135
Neistat's hand made
Evil Kneivel costume

Simon Owens has transformed his live/work space into a kind of crazy DIY art installation. Based in a back street in Dalston in East London, he works on the studio's ground floor. Here he created a giant wood box with removable walls filled with his props, books, strange objects, wires and electrical equipment. The rest of the creative room is littered with defunct pianos, retro furniture and wires. The breadth of his work has included everything from music promos to creating luxury wallets subtly emblazoned with swear words. He is currently working on film and TV concepts, an interior design project for a restaurant-come-gallery, and creative directing a record label.

Simon Owens

**FILMMAKER
DESIGNER**

LONDON

LOCATION
DALSTON

WWW
simonowens.com

IT'S PLACING THINGS IN A NEW CONTEXT. IF YOU GET IT RIGHT IT CAN BE VISUALLY VERY EXCITING

Working in so many mediums, what do you think unites your approach to design and creativity?
Dark humour, edge and beauty. Somewhere 'between the demonic and the miraculous'.

How did you start making films and promos?
I have, from an early age, been heavily into music videos. I would religiously record The Chart Show, America's Top 10, Dance Energy, The Word, Top of the Pops – anywhere there was music. My first commissioned music video was for Trevor Jackson's Playgroup. I had just started at the Royal College of Art. But because I was enjoying and loving what I was doing so much I just dropped out of the Royal College.

How long have you lived in your studio?
Five years. Originally we set up the space as 'The Imaginary Tennis Club'. Our own gallery, Millers Terrace, was on the ground floor at the front; 'The Imaginary Tennis Club' studio was at the back; and my living space upstairs was on the first floor. It is now just my studio on the ground floor, with me and my girlfriend living upstairs. When we eventually acquired the building, the ground floor was underwater! There was no heating or even electricity. The toilets didn't work. There wasn't a shower or bath facilities, not even stairs to get to the first floor. We had to climb up a ladder through a small trap door.

What was the story behind the Millers Terrace gallery?
This was started by myself, Nima Nourizadeh and Ash Lang. We then convinced a friend (Nicky Verber) to run the gallery day to day, and curate. After much work on the space, the gallery really took off. I designed all the graphics, organized bits and pieces. It was an incredibly exciting time. We would be making a video for Dizzee Rascal in the back while Nicky would be in the front talking to someone from the ICA.

Tell me about the studio box.
The box 'RABBITTRONIC WHEEEEL (AD JAMIE)' came from my obsession with things on wheels – the idea of mobiles, mobile libraries, caravans – combined with outsider art and something handmade. I wanted something that I felt represented me and was not your standard graphic design/production studio space. A great friend, Sven Ulber, who lives and works in Berlin, built it. He has this unique combination of skills and attitudes that are second to none. It took a lot of effort and time, as it was basically building a mini house on wheels. The front is three separate shelving units, which detach from the main part and can rest against the building walls, as if they were separate freestanding shelving units. It has pull-out drawers designed specifically with metal runners with a filing system inside. I wanted to use cheap, basic, utilitarian mass-produced materials. Both of us love OSB; it's a sort of particleboard, and can look slightly tropical.

How does the space reflect the work you make?
I think it's an idea or a concept. That's essentially what I'm about. I come up with lots of wild and fantastical ideas, and making my studio and living space this way was essentially the best way to present myself at the time.

Where did you find the other furniture in your home?
Some of it was given to me, some of it I found in the street – such as the armchair. Other things I searched for, such as the Ingmar Relling chair, Phillips lamp and the Bang & Olufsen television. I found my table in an architect's office in Berlin. The colourful, modular shelves that I use for DVDs and videos were bought from a pound shop for a Jack Penate video. The video didn't get put out in the end, but these stackable shelves have come to good use!

What are some of the weirdest objects you own?
I like my black African dolls, but I would say it is the whip that a 65-year-old granny left after one of my music videos (she was heavily into orgies and gang bangs). It's quite surreal thinking about her.

You use found objects in a lot of your work. What do you find interesting about that?
I like the fact they come from a different time and space, and sometimes have a history that I may not know. Perhaps you may not have liked it when it first appeared, but now, for all sorts of reasons, it makes sense. It's placing things in a new context. If you get it right it can be visually very exciting.

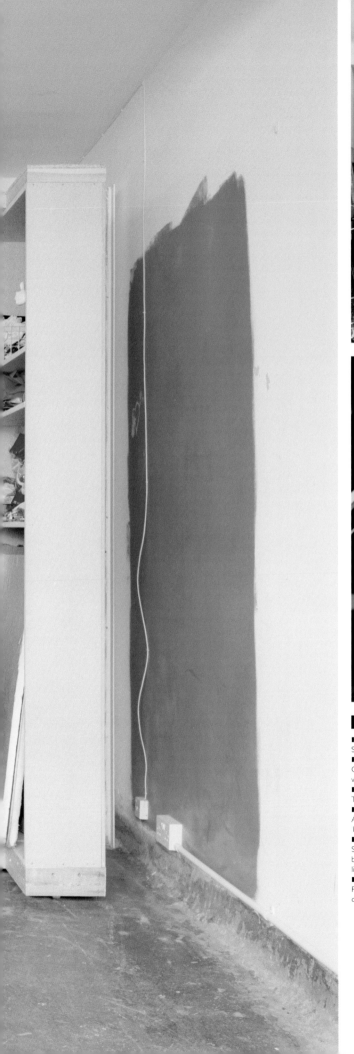

Page 137
Simon Owens
Page 138 & 139
Owens' handmade studio box –
with one removable wall open
Page 139 (top)
The studio box when closed
Page 139 (bottom)
A selection of Owens' collection of
1980s technology
Page 140
Shelving of open door of studio
box with materials, reference
library and toys
Page 141
Remnants of the building's murals and
old piano

Juan Redon

ARCHITECT
COLLECTOR
CURATOR
BARCELONA

LOCATION
EL BORNE
WWW
artium.org
colectania.es

I DON'T KNOW IF IT'S POSSIBLE TO TALK OF TASTE; I PREFER TO TALK ABOUT AN IDEA AND WHAT THAT IDEA IS

Architect, curator and pop collector Juan Redon's most creative project is the interior of his home. His flat, in a classic nineteenth-century block in the El Borne area of Barcelona, is literally crammed with art objects. There is no blank space in his home. Furniture by Philippe Starck, Jasper Morrison, Gio Ponti and Piero Fornasetti sits next to large-scale, often homoerotic, photography works by iconic artists including Jean-Baptiste Mondino, Andres Serrano, Richard Prince, John Waters, Rebecca Horn and David Byrne. The most striking objects in Redon's home are his obsessive collection of toys. On display next to outsider pop paintings by Gary Baseman and Manuel Ocampo or photos by Anton Corbijn are shelves filled with acres of Batmans, Supermans and Disney characters. Tables are covered in super-sized, limited-edition vinyl Qee and Bearbrick figures – often created by artists like KAWS or Pushead. Even Redon's kitchen objects feel like vitrines in a plastic museum. Redon has created a home that fulfils all his excessive, childhood fantasies.

What do you do?
I was born in Puerto de Sagunto, Valencia, in 1957. In 1973 I went to Madrid to study at the university. I'm an architect, and have lived in Barcelona since 1982 (more or less). I work on the reconstruction of old buildings in the old parts of cities. Barcelona, Palma de Mallorca, Bhaktapur in Nepal and Lima in Peru are the places where I'm working now. I also collect art. I gave a part of my collection of photography to the Artium Museum in Vitoria five years ago. Another part of my collection is in a private foundation, Foto Colectania.

Does your interior influence or reflect your work in any way?
Yes, I think so. I renovated this house for my partner and his family, and when they moved to Palma de Mallorca, I bought the flat. We were both art collectors, but with different tastes in art. I added the design furniture and the collection of toys. The actual house is very different from when my partner lived there.

Is Barcelona an influence on your space?
At this moment, no – definitely not. Maybe when I arrived in Barcelona, there was an atmosphere where design was important. All of the pieces of furniture I bought in Barcelona (except two or three pieces), but at the moment Barcelona brings to mind only Gaudí's Trencadís (Gaudí made some horrible things with little pieces of tails), cheap tourism and living sculptures on the Ramblas, the worst of the worst. I look to Paris, London and New York.

Your home is rammed with objects. What was the first thing you started collecting?
I don't remember; maybe when I was a child I collected comics, stamps… I say, 'when I have two pieces of something it's the start of a collection.' I started collecting art in 1993, when I moved to this house. I focused on photography particularly from 1996, and toys around the same time. I started buying Mickey Mouse and superheroes. Batman is my favourite. Another special toy for me is Atom or Astro Boy (depending on the Japanese or American name). During the last five years I began collecting adult toys from Japan and curated an exhibition in Barcelona called 'Red on Toyz'. Art Toys fuse toys and art. Normally I have the same toy painted in different designs by different artists. They are for adults, not for children.

What interests you about toys?
I love Pop Art, Andy Warhol and American pop culture. I'm interested in toys because they are beautiful, or I'm interested in the company that makes them. They never ask you anything and are the perfect companions to live with.

Tell me about your art collection. What were your first pieces?
The first piece in my collection was a painting by Pepe Nebot, a Spanish artist, and my first photography was a piece by Juan Pablo Ballester. Both are in my collection but are not on show in my home.

Do you think you have a specific aesthetic in your taste in art?
I don't know if it's possible to talk of taste; I prefer to talk about an idea and what that idea is.

There are a lot of boys in the pieces you own! What do you like about that imagery?
I'm gay and I like the boys and toys. There are a lot of boys in my collection. A good name for my collection is 'Boys and Toys'!

There's something overwhelming about your home. What appeals about that excess of objects?
There are too many things in my home. First was 'less is more', but I prefer 'more is less'. You are the king of your taste!

What are the most unusual things in your home?
The most unusual thing is my own home.

Page 143
Juan Redon
Page 144
A small part of Redon's toy collection
Page 145
Redon's kitchen shelves with more of
the toy collection
Pages 146 & 147
The apartment's living room
Page 147
Coffee table with Yoshitomo Nara
ashtray

Julia Schonlau

ILLUSTRATOR
CHARACTER DESIGNER
BERLIN

LOCATION
PRENZLAUER BERG
WWW
jujus-delivery.com

DOODLES ARE THE STARTING POINT TO EVERYTHING I CREATE

Julia Schonlau lives in a building overlooking a park to the north of Prenzlauer Berg, which is filled with East German interior details in addition to her own work, such as a skateboard emblazoned with illustrations. Her bedroom is painted yellow and filled with retro wooden furniture, as well as cupboards filled with her View-Master collection. In contrast, her work is often black, white and red – with echoes of children's books, classic tattoos and leftfield California-style comic books.

What is your background?
I studied photography and conceptual fine art but after I had graduated from college I immediately returned to the simplicity of drawing and became an illustrator and character designer. As I have no classical training in drawing and never went to a life drawing class, I had to find my own style.

How did you start doing illustration?
It's something I've always been doing. I first took it seriously when I did album covers, flyers, posters and merchandise for musician friends. In return they played for free at the opening of my first exhibition. We organized a joint concert and exhibition at Airport Tempelhof in Berlin.

How would you describe your approach to drawing?
Random doodles are usually the key to the best ideas. I don't want to control my drawings too much; I try to let my subconscious surprise me. The first sketch is maybe imperfect but usually the most expressive one. Doodles are the starting point to everything I create. Then I adapt them depending on the project. I sometimes work over them on the computer, make collages, screenprints, stencils and paint with acrylics.

What inspires your work?
Music is a big inspiration for me. All kinds of music, because it reflects different moods. I also love children's books from the 1960s, Japanese animation and I admire a lot of contemporary comic art.

Does Berlin inform what you do?
Berlin has not defined me as an artist or had any influence on my work, but it gave me the freedom to focus on doing my own thing. I can afford a studio. Whenever I want to do an exhibition, there is an abundance of alternative spaces to choose from. It's really about knowing what you're after, because everything is available here. Just recently I painted a petrol station from the 1920s with some friends. The petrol station is now a gallery that invites artists to make interventions onto the building.

How did you find your flat?
A friend of mine was already living in the house when I was flat-hunting and she gave me the number of her landlord. He showed me this flat, which was partly furnished. I chucked out the black wall units from the 1980s but kept the kitchen cupboard, two boxes of Christmas decorations from the GDR and a Russian dictionary.

Tell me about your View-Master collection.
I started collecting them when I was studying photography in England. At the time I was obsessed with charity shops and the objects that fascinated me most were kaleidoscopes and viewfinders. Whenever I saw one I had to pick it up, maybe because I never had one as a kid. My initial idea was to make my own reel for a viewfinder or one of those little plastic souvenir cameras. However, I didn't really want to take them apart, so instead I created a little sculpture with a viewfinder and an illuminated globe.

You have a lot of retro furniture. What appeals about it?
When I moved into this two-bedroom flat I had only a kitchen cupboard, which the previous owner had left behind, and a stool. So I asked my parents if they had any old stuff in the attic that I could have. Also I had inherited a bookcase from my grandfather, which I love a lot, because it reminds me of him. The rest I picked up from flea markets – there are two big ones just a few minutes from my house. The stuff there is really cheap, it's unique and the markets are close enough to carry the purchases home. I have one rule for furniture since I have moved so many times in my life: it has to be light, easy to take apart and if possible it should have wheels. What I like about old furniture is that you can't just go out and buy it – you have to find it.

You seem drawn to warm colours – yellow walls, warm wood.
Berlin can be very cold and grey in winter. And the winter lasts for a long time.

What are some of the most interesting or strange things in your space?
The coal ovens still fascinate me. When I moved in I had to carry coal up from the cellar, start a little fire with paper and wood and keep it going until the coals were glowing. I can't say it was fun, but it was like time-travelling, to experience something from a different era. Two years ago they put in central heating and I don't think I could go back. Most of the floor, ceiling and table lamps I own were made in the GDR. As I found out, the GDR did many great copies of classic sixties designs, which you could pick up dead cheap after the Wall had come down.

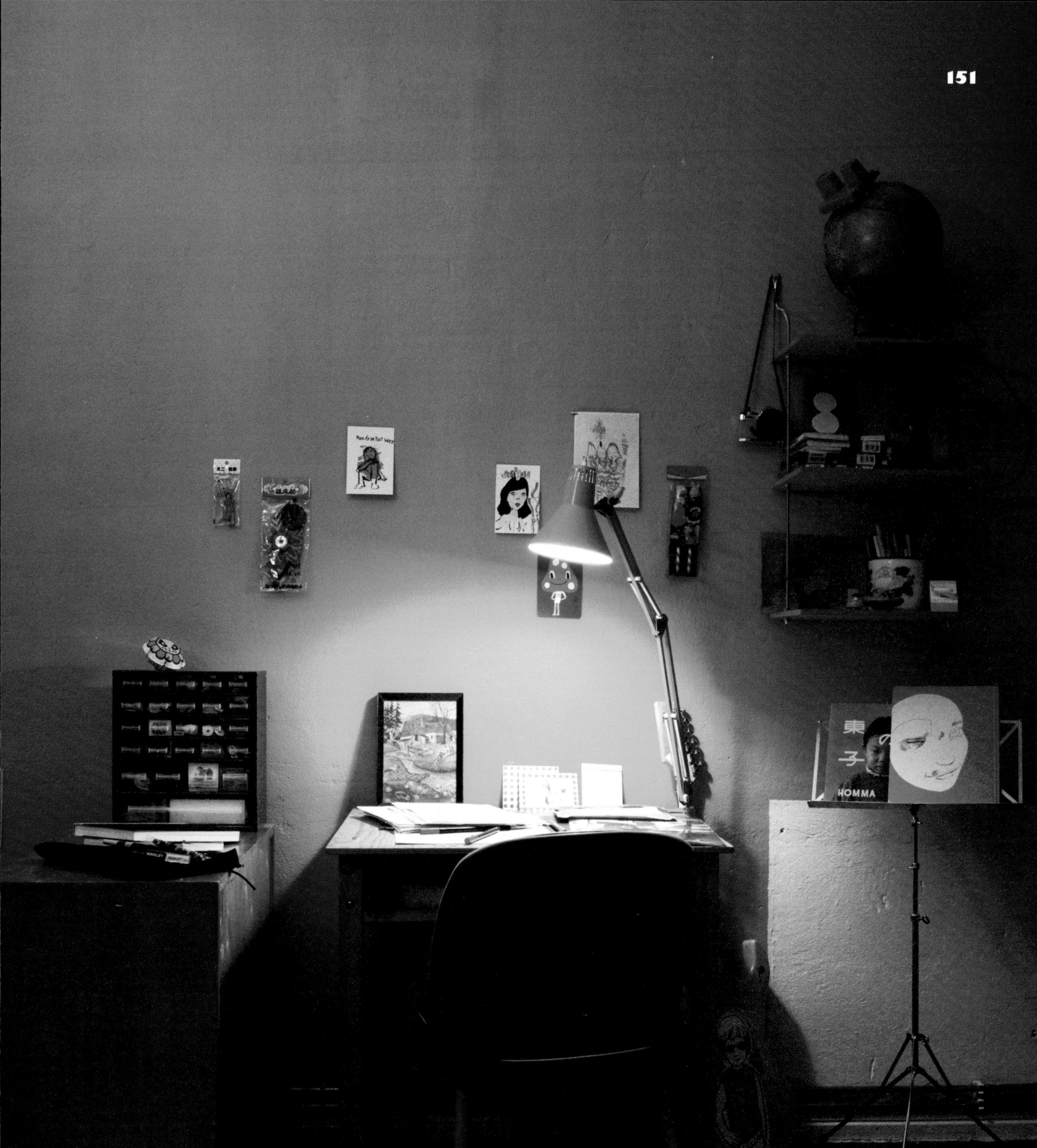
東
の
子
HOMMA

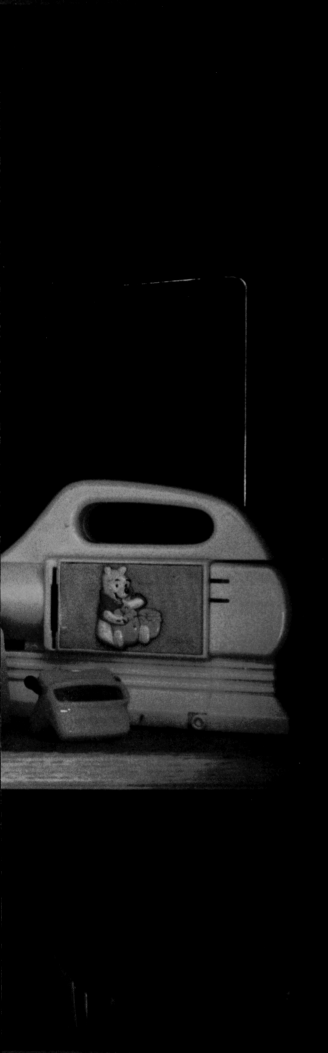

Stuart Semple

ARTIST

LONDON

LOCATION
ISLINGTON

WWW
stuartsemple.com

I TEND TO EITHER BE DRAWN TO REALLY INDUSTRIAL THINGS OR OLDER, MORE FANCY, THINGS; I LIKE THE HUMOUR IN THAT CONTRADICTION

Artist Stuart Semple's studio and home is like a small concrete aircraft hangar filled with easels, computers, iced cupcakes and art. The glass-fronted warehouse space overlooking a canal in Islington is split into two: the work studio largely downstairs and a domestic mezzanine space upstairs. Easels are positioned around the studio for Semple to move between. The artist's own work hangs next to his collection of plastic pop collectables and paintings. The studio reflects the magpie, graphic, pop approach of Semple's work. Something with touches of Warhol, fashion editorial and trash glamour.

Tell me about your working methods. You have numerous easels and workspaces around your home.
I like to have multiple things going on all the time, so I could be upstairs in my quiet drawing space and churn out things quite quickly. Or I could be downstairs with one of my painting easels, working on a piece that might last several months. I like to collect things and recombine them. Or write down song lyrics on the wall and move them round to different pieces I'm working on. I tend to accumulate piles and piles of magazines and books. I like to build an energy on one piece or in one area and then move to something else. I think that fluidity is important to me when I work. It keeps the brain going.

How do you differentiate between living and working spaces?
I suppose the mezzanine upstairs is my living area with my bed and kitchen, but even that is invaded by my drawing space. For some reason it feels like there's less pressure than working on them downstairs in the main studio space. I feel that I'm working until I get into bed.

Where did you find your furniture?
All over the place. When I first came to London, I had very little money and for the first few months I only had a couple of plastic chairs, then I got the very cheapest things from Ikea. Slowly as they've broken or I've grown out of them, I've replaced them. Often I like to get reconditioned things, or older things. My dining table was a Victorian worktable. My display cabinet was being chucked out of a clothes store. I rescued it and gave it a home. The old kitsch-looking chair that I sit on while drawing was a present from [the artist] Richard Galloway. I think his parents gave it to him from an old peoples' home. I tend to either be drawn to really

industrial things or older, more fancy, things; I like the humour in that contradiction.

Tell me about your cabinet of art and objects.
Quite often, when people visit, they give me little presents. It's almost a shrine to my friends and family. Most of the things in here were gifts. The Murakami toys came from my friend in Japan, the china cat from the artist David Hancock. I put one of those 1980s bricks of a mobile phone in there. I've got a bigger collection of those in storage. To me, that marks a change in the way things were, a time in the 1980s when the world shifted. I will probably be the last generation that will remember life before that stuff.

What's the story with the SEMPLE letters?
We did a project for the Art Car Boot Fair in 2007 and we had the DeLorean from *Back To the Future*; my friend the set designer Dave White made them out of foam to decorate the car and I decided to keep them. I love them as they are so perfect. They seem to have accumulated quite a lot of glitter now.

Tell me about some of the other art pieces you own.
Most are in storage until the day I have a space for them. I have a great painting here by Piers Secunda. I love the anti-Pop fragmentation of it; the fact the whole thing is constructed from moulded paint. I also have quite a large drawing collection. There are pieces by David Bray, Damien Hirst, Gavin Turk, Boo Saville, Maya Hewitt, Julian Opie, KAWS and many others.

How does your space influence your work?
Most of my inspiration comes from man-made images, so the studio has become a bit of a container or storage house for them. That's why I need so many computers in the office area. There are four G5s in there full of imagery I've collected over a decade. In my work, I collect fragments or residue of mass visual culture and put them together. I think the studio is a bit like that too – quite disparate things coming together.

How does the concreteness of the studio affect your approach to its interior?
It's very hard to decorate, because I never know what I'll need to do next in here. I might suddenly need the whole thing for a massive painting or the whole floor to make a multiple or something. I think it's forced me to decorate with clusters of small objects; to put my personality on the space in more subtle ways. I get bored if things are too static.

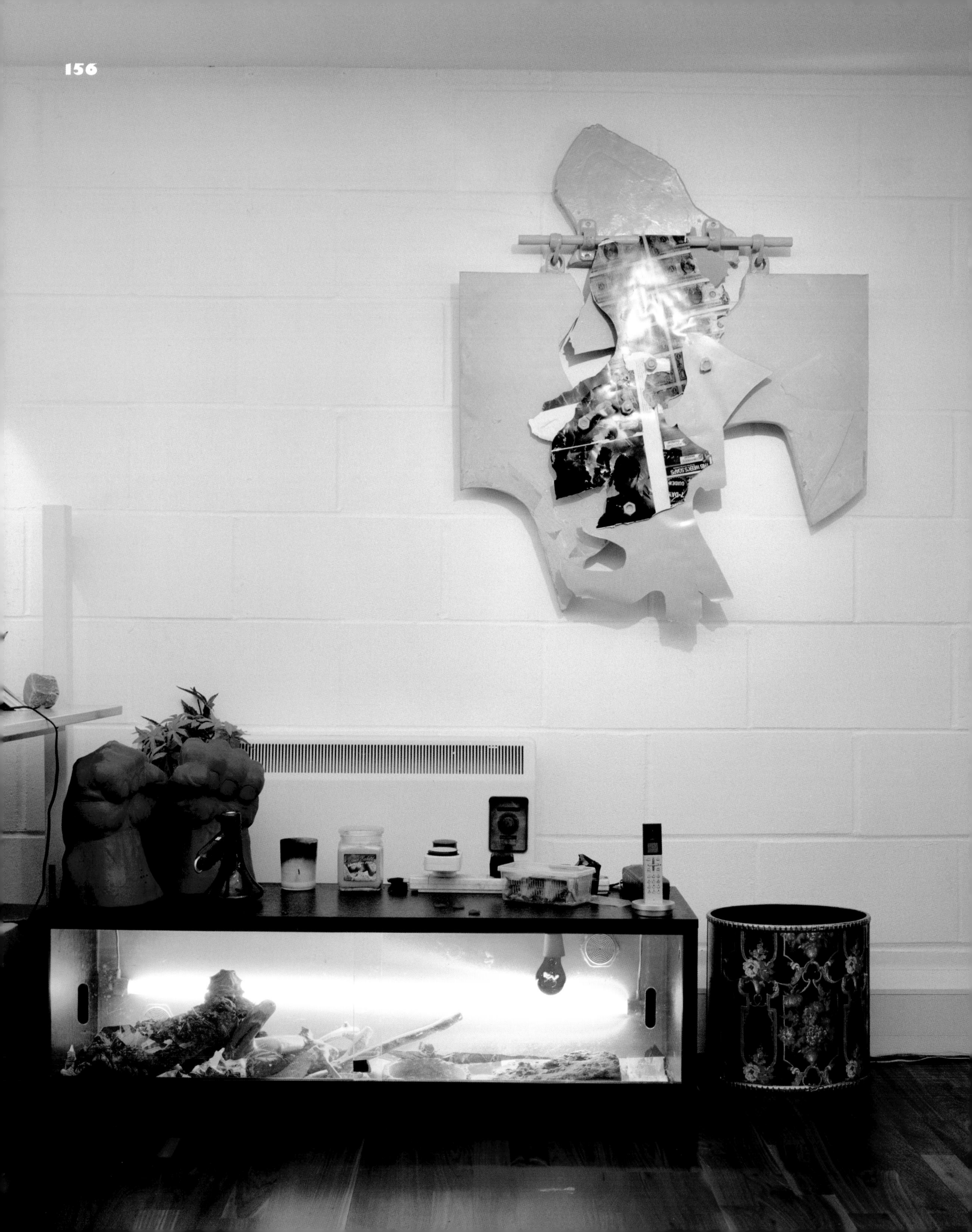

Snakeskin Jacket

SET, PROP AND FURNITURE DESIGNERS
LONDON

LOCATION
SMITHFIELDS
WWW
myspace.com/swaparamarazzmatazz

WE HAD A CRUCIFIED RUBBER SKELETON WITH A FAIRY LIGHT CROWN FOR A CHRISTMAS TREE

Henry Armand Smith and Dean Slydell are Snakeskin Jacket, a duo that has worked on props, sets, furniture and events for Vivienne Westwood, Eley Kishimoto, Wound Magazine, Maison Bertaux and various directors for TV, film and music videos. Their home in Smithfields veers between brilliance and chaos the minute you walk in the door – past the broken piano that is crammed on its side next to the stairwell. There is nothing humdrum about the space. In one corner of the central living room, a bedroom was created out of cardboard boxes and coloured panes of Perspex. The opposite side of the room is like a pastiche of a nineteenth-century drinking club. The space is as varied and unpredictable as the work the pair creates.

How did you form Snakeskin Jacket?
We are old friends and about four years ago began working together doing the sets and art direction on music videos for the director Nick Frew. When we moved into the building we found ourselves in a position to have a great workshop so we branched out and started producing other bits and bobs. Snakeskin Jacket was the company we formed; a nod to Nick Cage in the film *Wild at Heart;* 'This here jacket represents a symbol of my individuality, and my belief in personal freedom.'

You've done a lot of different projects – from Happy Mondays music videos to sets for Vivienne Westwood shows – what links your approach?
Saying yes to everything we get asked to do! Between us, and a pool of talent we have worked with in the past, we have found with a bit of thought and pre-planning we can always solve most problems. This way you get to learn new processes and techniques that you can later apply to other jobs.

Tell me about the furniture you've made.
We have made furniture for parties, film props, restaurants and showrooms. The materials vary, often with a leaning towards the recycled. As we enjoy making these bits, we often tend to take this route rather than hiring or buying new.

How did you end up living in the space?
A good friend, Robert Pinnock, put us onto the space. It's basically looking after empty buildings for developers or companies. We had a call from Robert one day saying 'get to Smithfields and bring a sleeping bag'. We got there, secured the building and began turning it into our space.

There are Eley Kishimoto prints around the space, especially the bathroom filled with fake surveillance cameras. How did that happen?
Mark Eley wanted to use the space as his showroom during 2006 fashion week. We had only just moved back in, as the site had been the HQ for the London Architecture Biennale for a month. When we moved back, the space was empty again so we had a clean slate. We needed a toilet/shower and kitchen, so when Mark approached us, we jumped at the chance, knowing we could source some great materials off him. His printed plywood and plasterboard were fantastic. We had seen it before and knew he would have some bits around his studio. The surveillance cameras were sitting around in the workshop. We thought it would be unnerving to fit them in the bathroom! No one likes being watched on the toilet!

How did your Victorian corner evolve?
We call it 'Gentleman's Corner'. It's just collections of found objects and props we have gotten for music videos and various jobs. We decided to make the corner as decoration for an evening we host called 'The Boys Club', where a variety of our friends come for dinner to talk, drink, and get away from girls for the evening.

What's the story behind the Swap-A-Rama Razzmatazz sign?
Swap-A-Rama Razzmatazz is a party we started with the concept of attending the night in the clothes that are in the bottom of your wardrobe that you don't wear anymore. Throughout the night we ring a klaxon, when everyone must swap an item of clothing. We all agreed we needed a swap box, the concept of this being a bright noisy object that signalled to the audience when it was time to swap clothes.

How did you end up making a room out of cardboard boxes for Intersection magazine's creative director Yorgo Tloupas?
A friend of ours, the shoe designer Nicholas Kirkwood, needed a place to store his next season's shoeboxes. We agreed, not quite understanding how many boxes we were going to receive. Yorgo Tloupas moved in, and one evening we found ourselves building his room.

Where did you find the objects in your space?
Anywhere and everywhere. Skips, household waste sites, streets. If we find something interesting and can get it home any way possible, we do.

Does your space reflect your work?
The space is our work. When you live in a temporary place you need to create the living space to be versatile and moveable. Shelves and walls are made from reclaimed wood, which is not great to look at, so the best thing is to decorate them with our interesting collected bits.

What is the strangest object in your home?
The Broken Boudoir Grand Piano at the bottom of the stairs, which was used in a music video. We never could face hauling it up to the living space, though. The bed is made from scaffolding. I bought an expensive mattress, but didn't have the funds to buy a bed frame, so we made it from dirty old scaffold poles. We had a crucified rubber skeleton with a fairy light crown for a Christmas tree.

Page 161
Henry Armand Smith and Dean
Slydell, a.k.a. Snakeskin Jacket
Pages 162 & 163
Detail of living space with its found
furniture
Page 163
Items in the Gentlemen's Corner

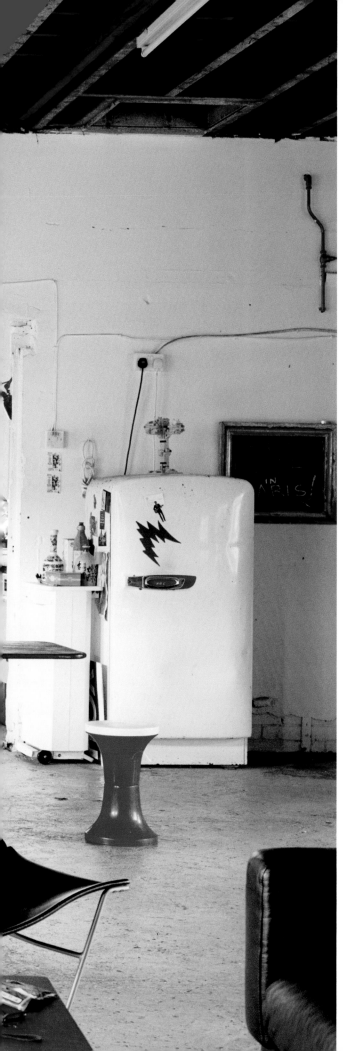

Aya Takano

Japanese artist Aya Takano is a protégé of international art sensation Takashi Murakami. Her haunting paintings, however, have a very different feel from Murakami's hyper-pop aesthetic. Instead, she depicts naked girls floating around space with bug eyes, or wandering through disturbing spaces in a psychedelic urban landscape. There's something both sexual and innocent about the female characters that populate her paintings. The work is more mesmerising than the average expression of Japanese kawaii, or cuteness.

Takano lives on the outskirts of Tokyo in an industrial warehouse area overlooking the sea. She works and lives in a high-ceilinged studio apartment with textured raw concrete walls. A quarter of the space is devoted to her black pug dog, who lives next to her paintings in progress. The apartment is typically Tokyo-tiny, but doesn't feel it. Inspirational odds and ends – notably Takano's alien toys and pictures – are littered on shelves and tables. Alongside her artwork, Takano has written about science fiction. The studio, with its view of the city's industrial landscape, feels like a lo-fi take on space-age futurism.

How did you first become involved with Kaikai Kiki?
When I was a university student, I found an ad for an internship with Takashi Murakami. I thought that it would be a great opportunity to witness his work process. So I started working for him as an intern. Then, when I heard that he was seeing young artists' works, I took a chance and showed him my art. He liked it and soon became my producer.

Your paintings are filled with colour – what attracts you to that?
Thank you for saying so. I don't think my paintings are filled with colour. I wish they were. I like watching clouds. They have such nice colours and their colours are changing every minute. It's fascinating. I hope I could paint something like that.

How long have you been living in your apartment?
Since autumn 2006. My space is beautiful. I can see the big bridge and fireworks. It has a high ceiling. It's simple and functional. Also, I like the fact that it's located near the sea.

ARTIST
TOKYO

LOCATION
ODAIBA
WWW
kaikaikiki.co.jp

I CAN SEE SO MANY DIFFERENT SHAPES, LOOKING AT THAT WALL

It's in a very industrial area on the outskirts of Tokyo. What appealed to you about that location?
Location didn't matter to me when I was looking for a space. My only concern was ceilings. I need high ceilings to produce my work. So I ended up here and it's actually quite a fun place.

As you work in the space as well as live in it, how do you think the apartment influences your paintings?
It makes my life easier because I don't need to move from the house to the studio. Also, I like doing several things at the same time, so working at home suits me well.

The apartment itself has got great concrete walls. What do you like about that bareness?
A lot of foreigners are surprised when they see these bare concrete walls, but I think Japanese people see this kind of wall as modern and cool. It might be the influence of Tadao Ando. I like its rustic appearance. I can see so many different shapes, looking at that wall.

When did you first become interested in aliens?
When I was a kid. The books my father read influenced me. Space is super-vast, so it's strange to think there aren't any aliens somewhere out there. I would like to know how they think differently from human beings. I would like to meet them.

Where do you collect the toys and alien things in your home?
Nerdy fan shops in Tokyo, small second-hand shops outside Tokyo, or online.

Does the paper clock above your bed actually work?
It does. I like it because it looks just like paper, just as you thought.

What is the most unusual object in your home?
Maybe the certificate of ownership of a piece of land on the moon? I own one acre. It was a present!

Where do you find your furniture? You have some unusual pieces, like the seat made from an old skateboard and the small sofa.
I find them in many different places. As for the skateboard seat, I bought it at GEISAI (an event organized by Murakami). It was made by a self-taught furniture designer. Japanese houses are small, so I think you can easily find small sofas in a lot of furniture shops. I bought mine at the shop called Unico.

Nakano Tsuyoshi

True creatives like Nakano Tsuyoshi are unrestricted by mediums. Nakano founded the ngap brand – a wide-reaching project that has grown from streetwear into a multi-product label. ngap products range from furniture to textile design to menswear. Nakano has a very creative approach to interiors, fusing traditional Japanese and Chinese methods of making furniture with a whimsical sense of humour. His objects have included a drunken stool printed with a graphic demonstrating drunken footsteps like dance steps. He made a metal 'Fopoon' – a spoon with fork teeth attached. He made a giant bed that resembles an oversized, canvas holdall, and a table and set of stools that look like wrapped-up packages made out of worn brown leather.

Apart from his own work, Nakano has worked with cult fashion designer Jun Takahashi. He created one incarnation of the interior of the flagship store for Takahashi's fashion label Undercover. The results are very memorable, bridging the space between punk, interior design and sculpture. Nakano proclaimed at the time in A magazine, 'You gonna see products you've never seen before.'

Collaborative pieces include a sofa called the UHH & NAA Rockin' Chair. The piece was a kind of homage to the desert. The pale leather two-seater had a rocking-chair base and was covered in woven blankets. Each arm of the sofa had on it a leather sculptural head of a camel wearing sunglasses. In another project, an Eames chair was amended to have a giant 'A for anarchy' symbol as its backrest.

There is a creative independence in Nakano's approach to everything. He also co-owns CREEPS, a studio and gallery space filled with his signature designs. His home is crammed with objects, artworks and a unique sense of freedom.

How would you sum up what you do?
Creation.

How did you set up ngap and where did the name come from?
It stands for 'N&G action paint'. Me, N for Nakano, and my partner G got our training doing decorating together, hanging out in Harajuku and getting random job offers. ngap has been going for 15 years now. G has left for Nishiomote Island – an island the furthest south in Japan. He's running N&G action farm (ngaf) growing mangos, pineapples, papayas and vegetables. And I'm working in Tokyo! We believe that we will be able to join those two projects, so I'm working hard every day to make it happen and have a good NG life.

Is a sense of Japanese-ness important to your work?
Of course it is important to me. I was born Japanese and grew up in Japan so the Japanese element is naturally included in all my creations.

You've created interiors for shops and studios. How does that influence your own space?
It is actually the opposite. ngap, my own space, influences what I make outside.

How do you approach making your furniture?
I always try to make something you can use to really chill out and relax.

There's a lot of humour in your pieces. What do you like about that?
I like the moment when I can laugh at what I make.

What do you like about creating things in so many different mediums?
I can see many different facets of my materials by using different mediums. I like touching them and finding a different use for each of them.

You created these fake wood bricks. What are they actually made of? How did you come up with the idea?
It is made of wood. Gymnastics halls inspired me. I used brand new wood and painted it to make it look like a gymnastics hall floor. It's applying the same idea as d.n.o. chair (do not open). The ones you saw at my place.

How long have you been in the space in Harajuku? What do you like about it?
For 15 years. It is always an exciting place.

FOUNDER OF NGAP, FASHION, FURNITURE, INTERIOR AND PRODUCT DESIGNER

TOKYO

LOCATION
HARAJUKU

WWW
creeps.jp

I LIKE THE MOMENT WHEN I CAN LAUGH AT WHAT I MAKE

You have Phil Frost and Doze Green artworks on the wall. How did you get them?
My friends brought those artists here, to ngap, and they painted the artworks while they were here.

You have quite a lot of African or North African pieces in your place. Do you find a lot of things while travelling?
Yes; I travelled to Morocco in 2004 and to Senegal in 2006.

Page 175
Nakano Tsuyoshi
Page 176
'Wrapped up package' leather seats
near the studio entrance
Page 177
Nakano's glove and mask collection
Pages 178 & 179
View of the main living/workspace
with Tsuyoshi's leather 'wrapped up
package' seats and table in the
foreground
Page 179
Items on Nakano's desk

Julie Verhoeven

ARTIST

LONDON

LOCATION
PECKHAM

WWW
riflemaker.org

I LOVE THE FEELING OF ATTACKING THE SPACE WITH COLOUR AND PATTERN, KNOWING IT'S ALL LIABLE TO GO WRONG

Julie Verhoeven is the kind of creative eccentric that only Britain could produce. The artist, illustrator and fashion designer creates fluid artworks that have a unique sense of theatricality and eroticism, as well as decorative flourish. Her home in south London is quirky and unusual. The banisters of the stairs are covered with coloured vinyl strips. Most of her walls have swathes of colour or pattern. The narrow house seems to have evolved organically. As things have worn out, Verhoeven creatively patches them with colour and pattern – making their disintegration a point of chaotic inspiration.

Did your work grow out of fashion or illustration?
It grew from drawing fashion dollies with huge cleavages from an early age.

How does your work relate to fashion?
My background and day job is fashion and as much as I try to move away from it, I cannot deny I love it. It informs everything I do. I teach womenswear at MA level at Central Saint Martins and the Royal College of Art. I am drawn to the theatrics, pantomime and absurdity of it all. It's often a spectacle. However, it's a deadly serious industry, which I greatly respect and now begin to feel proud to have been involved in. I take great joy from dressing up and dressing others. I also have a love–hate relationship with the speed at which the industry moves. I am constantly being driven to look ahead and keep up. This need to keep looking and observing really ignites my drawing. Arriving at the art world relatively late, it seemed idiotic not to allow my fashion roots out in some form or other, which is partly why I am beginning to execute crude pieces in 3D again.

A lot of your work came out of drawings but are moving more towards sculpture or installation. What do you like about that sense of 3D?
Everything begins with a drawing for me, or is rooted there. The move into installation and sculpture satisfies the less polite and more showy-offy side of me. I like to dip into an area I often consider to be very masculine and smug. I like to produce apparent nonsense.

How did you end up in your home?
I followed my brother to Camberwell and started to rent. Then I got too comfortable and bought the flat.

How have you changed the space?
The main change was stripping the flat of the cruddy carpet and letting rip with coloured paint and coloured vinyl – until no surface was left untouched.

How has your home's décor changed and developed over the years?
As it's become scruffier, dog-eared and crumbling, it's gained vinyl layers, paint shapes and blobs. When I wore out the floor where I sit in the living room, I splashed enamel paint puddles over the scuff marks. Colour-wise, it's moving from louder and louder to darker and 'adult'. I purposely threw black paint over the coloured striped wall to upset the rhythm. I painted the bedroom dark, traditional, stately-home colours, but very badly, leaving the chipwood ceiling horror – which I have grown attached to.

What are some of the stranger objects in your home?
A pair of outsize crutches and a plaster polar bear with a whisk-head, disguised as a toilet attendant.

What are some of the things you've made for your home?
A wadded cosy footstool, with an extra child's leg protruding from it (a mini Robert Gober soft furnishing homage) and a two-metre-long outsized plimsoll doorstop. The 1990s BT home phone wrapped in parcel tape always attracts attention.

How do you think your own artworks sit in your home?
Often they are white, which is an interesting contrast to a place that is full of colour and pattern. I like to test-run the pieces in the flat, to live with them for a bit. I resist producing them in colour, as they somehow appear otherworldly in white. I like to kid myself that they have more integrity in white and might be taken more seriously.

Your walls are covered in a lot of pattern and colour. What do you like about that approach?
I love the feeling of attacking the space with colour and pattern, knowing it's all liable to go wrong. I love to work with happy accidents. I like the crassness and arrogance of such a decision.

Is there a relationship between your home and your work?
I need the security of a home surrounded by invigorating or warm colours, shapes and surplus nonsense, in order to produce work with a calm head. A contradiction, perhaps?

How do you think London informs your work?
I love the noise of the road and the tension. I need to maintain the sense that everything is moving fast, and I need to keep up.

Tell me about your collaged bathroom.
The avocado bathroom suite informed the décor in the bathroom. I decided to wholeheartedly embrace this classic and celebrate it by collaging every surface in vinyl of all shades of green and jade. I believe it is the smallest bathroom in the UK. There is no point denying it, so I just made it appear super-busy with pattern.

Page 181
Julie Verhoeven
Pages 182 & 183
Verhoeven's living room walls and shelving
Page 183 (top)
Coffee table with part of Verhoeven's collection of retro magazines
Page 183 (bottom)
Artworks by Verhoeven

Corliss Elizabeth Williams

GRAPHIC DESIGNER, ONLINE BOUTIQUE OWNER

NEW YORK

LOCATION
BROOKLYN

WWW
glitterminivintage.com

IT'S HARD FOR ME TO PART WITH THINGS LIKE PLASTIC FARM ANIMALS, MANNEQUIN HEADS, RANDOM FLIERS...

Michigan-born Corliss Elizabeth Williams has been living in New York City for a decade. Williams began as an assistant to the creative director at the New York Times magazine before freelancing in editorial design. She is currently assistant art director at Time magazine. Her second life is as the owner of online vintage clothing store Glittermini, and her home in Brooklyn reflects this double life. It is based largely around the living room/bedroom, which is split by a large shelf. Design books sit next to disused clocks, worn-out toys and retro furniture. Giant typewriting posters hang alongside masturbating toy soldiers and transvestite dolls. Somehow, the bright yellow space manages to be quirky but not overtly cluttered.

What first drew you to graphic design?
I have always been considered the 'arty' one in my family, and I would always spend my allowance on all of the magazines, books and art supplies that I could find. I struggled in maths and science in school, and would always opt out of writing long boring papers for an English class, and create things like castles or puppets to express myself. I decided to go to Pratt Institute, where I got my BFA in Communications Design in Graphic Design.

How would you describe your aesthetic approach?
Before tackling any design project, I take a look at the world around me, books on the subject of what I am hoping to get influenced by, and most importantly, I sketch out my ideas, and talk them out with friends. I marinate my ideas, and then I go from there.

Tell me more about your interest in vintage fashion.
I presently run an online clothing store, Glittermini Vintage. I get clothes from various Salvation Army stores and friends who want to put their items up in the store and sell them online. Most of my buyers seem to be from Australia or Brooklyn. I get a kick out of buying something pretty and being able to share it with someone else. Clothes are meant to be shared, in my opinion. My dream is to run my own reasonably priced vintage store to keep all of the ladies of the world sophisticated and chic.

When did you first move into the apartment?
I moved in to my apartment in July 2006. I moved from a much larger brownstone in Brooklyn where I had a number of pieces of furniture that I didn't think I'd be able to bring with me. But I got very lucky – the studio that I found was more like a small one-bedroom. The guy who lived there before me left me his bookshelf, which acted perfectly as a divider, creating a living space and a sleeping area.

How did you approach filling the space?
I'm horrible at throwing things away, so it's hard for me to part with things like plastic farm animals, mannequin heads, random fliers, and other found objects that I come across.

Unusually, you've gotten lots of objects from Craig's List.
Craig's List is like a virtual flea market. You can come across a ton of junk, or treasures. It's all a matter of looking and hitting the jackpot. I don't have much money to spend on fancy brand new furniture right now, so I discovered Craig's List a couple of years ago.

What objects did you get from it?
I got my orange couch, the teal hutch, my bicycle, kitchen table and chairs, clocks, air conditioner, and I've also gotten rid of things too. When I do deep spring cleaning, I'll create a 'come and get this free box of stuff' listing.

What are the strangest things you have in your home?
I recently got a giant typing-class poster from the 1970s from my father from when he taught typing in high school. It's huge and is in my kitchen. It takes up the entire wall.

Tell me about the toys in your home – particularly the strange doll cake decorations.
I love those things! I got them at an arts and crafts store back home in Michigan. I just thought they were so strange. They were these topless little dolls in a bag with messed-up hair. I thought that they'd look much better nailed to my wall rather than dressed up in frosting on top of a cupcake. The next thing that I really want is a mannequin arm or leg. I already have a head that I can put different hairpieces on, my two Hawaiian busts and my dress form, but I need another object to help me complete my collection!

There are a lot of velvet details in your home. What interests you about texture?
My apartment is certainly texture-driven. Every piece of furniture stands alone – the distressed painted wood hutch, the slickly painted steel TV stand, my velvet couch. Somehow they all seem to go together, and my apartment is definitely a quirky, fun reflection of who I am.

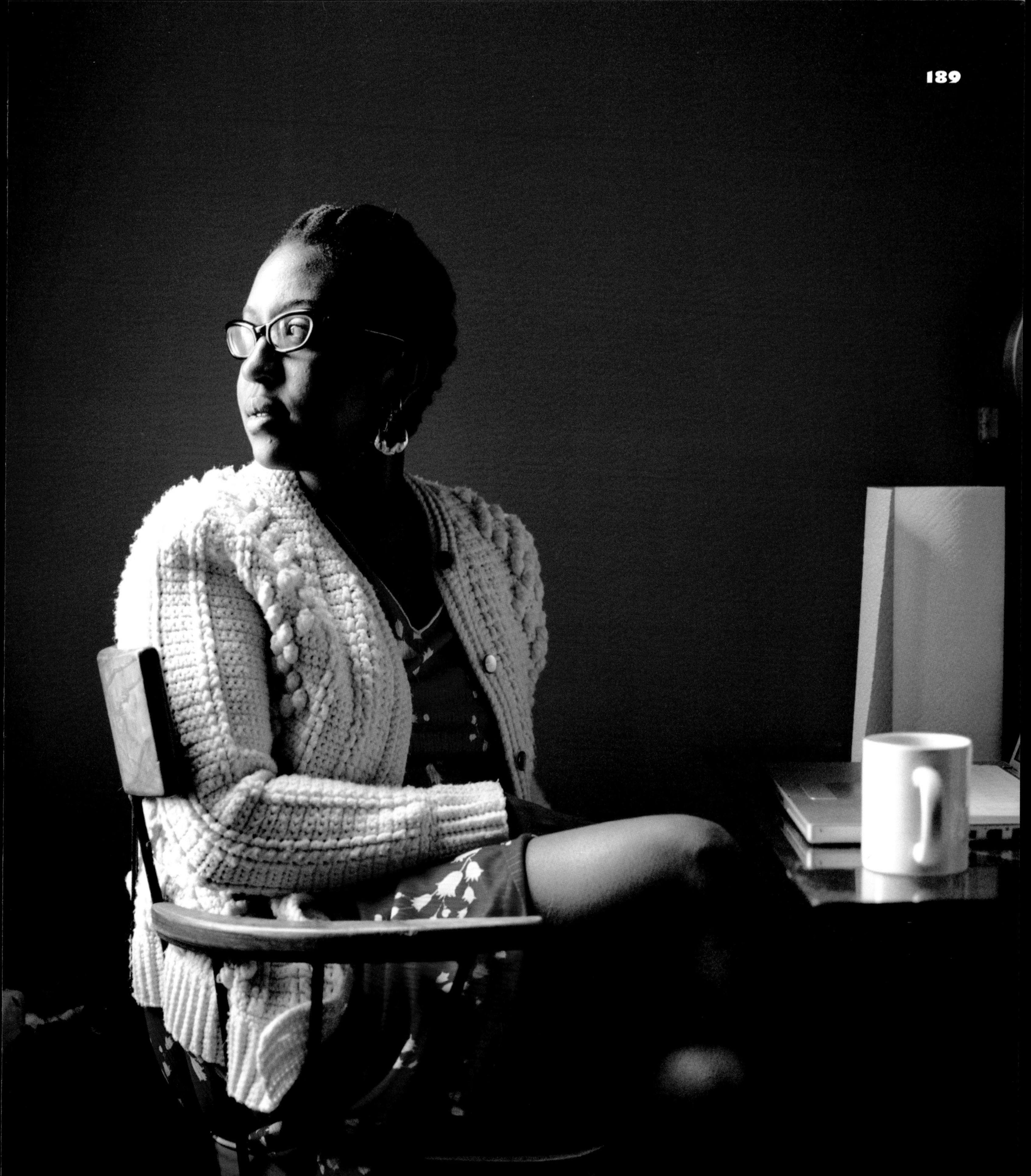

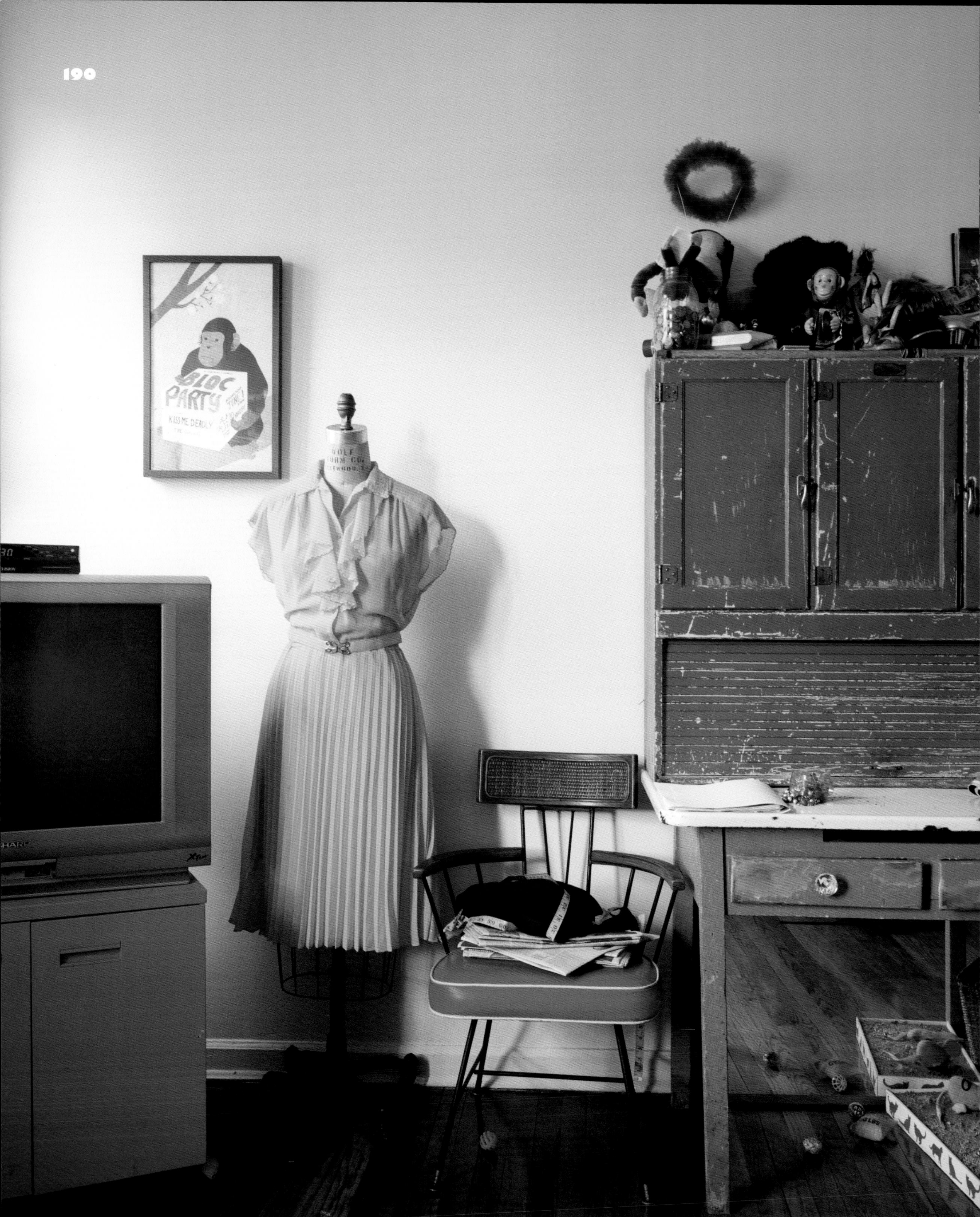
BLOC
PARTY
KISS ME DEADLY
WOLF
FORM CO.

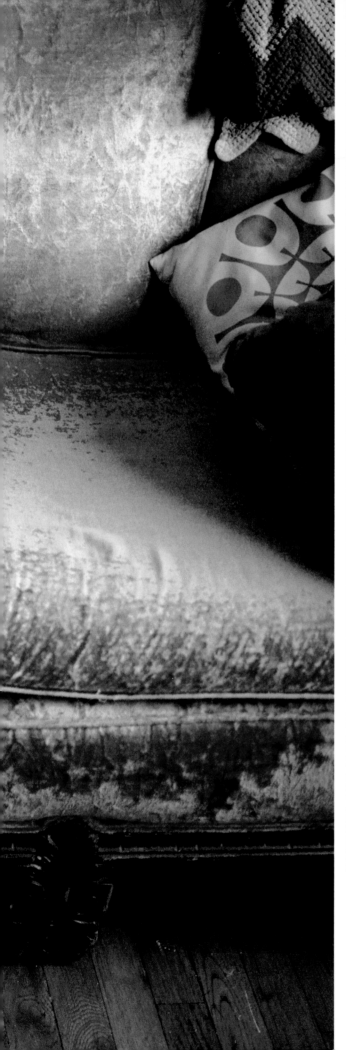

Page 189
Corliss Elizabeth Williams
Page 190
The living space near the entrance to
Williams' apartment
Page 191
View of the sofa from Craig's List and
desk in the living space
Pages 192 & 193
Detail of sofa
Page 193 (top)
Framed retro magazine images
Page 193 (bottom)
Shelving and toys

Yasumasa Yonehara

Yasumasa Yonehara, a.k.a. Yone, is something of a phenomenon in Japan. He began as an editor on style and teen magazines, which led to editing books on amateur photography. When he started taking his own photographs of sexy young women – on a small-scale Polaroid-like Fuji camera – his work developed a massive following. Now he's a celebrity, with women lining up for him to photograph them for international exhibitions and art books. Visually, his work has a similar playful approach to Terry Richardson, rather than the intensity of Araki. He argues that the work is really dictated by the women, who collaborate on the images with Yone during shoots. Although sexual, the work is intended to be more about the women's desire than the photographer's own objectification. Yone's second home in Tokyo is a boy's fantasy – rammed with books, toys, CDs, videos, discarded photographs of half-naked women and artworks by major graffiti artists. There's a hecticness and chaos to the space – a reflection of Yone's crazy, creative life.

**PHOTOGRAPHER
CURATOR
EDITOR**

TOKYO

LOCATION
MEGURO

WWW
loveyone.blogspot.com

THE PLACE BECAME MY SECOND HOUSE: A PLACE FOR MY HOBBIES, MY PLAYGROUND

Tell me about how you use the space. You call it your 'nightime studio'?
When I first started using this space, it was more of a studio and an office. But after renting another place as a photographic studio five years ago, the place became my second house: a place for my hobbies, my playground. I often end up sleeping there after partying hard with my friends and getting drunk. It is very close to the house where I live with my family. Because of that, I feel safe and secure here. That's why I stay here often, I guess.

How did you first find the apartment?
I found it 13 years ago. My friends' rap group Schadaraparr and a few photographer friends were living there.

You have a massive book collection here. Do you use them as inspiration?
I can sense which books will go out of print, even when the content or the design is good. You can find a lot of books on my shelves that aren't available any more, or that have now become very expensive. I also like buying bestsellers after the hype around them has expired. I think that books that sold millions of copies illustrate a certain period of time really well. It's really interesting to read them. From the former, I learn originality, and from the latter I learn ordinary thinking.

You began as an editor and curator. How do you feel that influenced your work when you became a photographer?
I still consider myself an editor and curator rather than a photographer. My interest in photography is not to demonstrate how good or bad my work is. It is about editing methods.

Your work is about the relationship between you and the young women you photograph. Rather than just your point of view, the images reflect how the women want to present themselves. What do you find interesting about that relationship?
I'd be so happy if you thought that was my approach. Taking photos according to girls' desires is high-quality documentation.

Tell me about your toys. There are a lot of monsters in your collection.
I collect toys that are either extremely gross or extremely cute – or are of girls.

Tell me about some of the artworks in your space. How did you get the pieces on advertising signs by Delta and Futura?
When sex lines became really popular, these illegal ads called *sutekan* started appearing everywhere. 'Sutekan' literally means 'throw-away ads'. You would find them pasted on the electricity poles all over Tokyo. I got really attracted to their Pop aesthetic, so whenever I found a well-designed *sutekan*, I would take it home with me. When artists visited me in here, they would always get interested in *sutekan*, and want to use them for their own work. These artists would transform these ads while I was telling them the *sutekan* Tokyo story.

You have a framed portrait of Terry Richardson. What kind of relationship do you think there is between your work and his?
I got to know him when he came to Japan for his exhibition at Hysteric Glamour about ten years ago. He came to my office every night and we discussed our philosophy of looking at sexy photos. We share a very similar way of capturing the subject. I think we are like-minded.

There's a speed to the way you approach taking photos. What do you like about that freedom and immediacy?
I push the shutter not according to my will, but the models' will.

What do you like about the chaos of your space?
It may look chaotic but I know where everything is.

Does the space influence or inspire your work at all?
I guess it is more a place to present my works and my tastes to my friends.

MAGICIAN
MAGIC RACER
GLO DINO
LOST IN SPACE
Violator Chopper
MY WIFE
男性用無料案内
03-5272-2222
03-5463-9090
BRING ME YOUR LOVE
CHARLES BUKOWSKI

Page 195
Yasumasa Yonehara
Pages 196 & 197
A small selection of the shelving in
Yonehara's studio
Pages 198 & 199
Items on the living space floor
Page 199 (top & bottom)
Detail of objects on Yonehara's shelves

Pages 200 & 201
Framed photographs near the
window

Page 201
Detail of shelving

Barcelona

AREA
EL BORNE

This laid-back area to the east of the Ramblas is very popular with the city's creatives, escaping the tourist hoards. The area is filled with cafés, bars, design shops, one-off boutiques and tapas bars.

SHOPPING
VALLERY

Calabria 85, 08015 Barcelona
(+34 935 396 430; www.vallery.es)
A great gallery and shop that stocks unusual graphic and design objects, clothing, zines, prints, toys and general cool stuff.

INTERIOR SHOPPING
PILE 43

c. Agla, 4, Barri Gòtic, 08002 Barcelona
Only in Barcelona would you get a furniture store and cocktail bar in one. This place, open only in the evenings, sells tons of vintage furniture and lights, as well as the best mojitos in town.

GALLERY
IGUAPOP

Comerç, 15, 08003 Barcelona
(+34 933 100 735; www.iguapop.net)
Iguapop is one of the best outsider art galleries in the world, with changing shows by leftfield names like Gary Baseman, Gary Taxali and Kim Gordon. Check their very impressive affiliated music programme, which has put on bands from Feist to Nirvana.

COFFEE
CAFÉ C3

Montalegre, 5, 08001 Barcelona
(+34 933 064 100; www.cccb.org)
This terrace café is hidden by gallery (and skate) Mecca CCCB. A secret suntrap, with a good vegetarian menu.

FOOD
CAFÉ DE L'ACADEMIA

c. Lledo, 1, Barri Gòtic, 08002 Barcelona
(+34 933 150 026)
This popular restaurant specializes in very authentic Catalan food at surprisingly reasonable prices. Grab the three-course set lunch on the terrace in summer. Open weekdays only.

DRINK
GIMLET

c. Rec, 24, Borne, 08021 Barcelona
(+34 933 101 027)
This very classic cocktail bar in Borne, with standing room only, exudes old-school charm. Good for a relaxed drink to start off the night.

CLUB
SALA APOLO

c. Nou de la Rambla 113, 08004 Barcelona
(+34 934 414 001; www.sala-apolo.com)
The best live music venue in Barcelona hosts any major act coming through town, as well as putting on changing club nights.

HOTEL
CHIC& BASIC

c. Princesa, 50, 08003 Barcelona
(+34 932 954 652; www.chicandbasic.com)
This boutique hotel in Borne is a minimalist's dream. The lovely, completely white rooms have coloured lights that can change at the touch of button. The epitome of refreshing.

Berlin

AREA

KREUZBERG

This area in south-east Berlin is lively, gritty and has a thriving Turkish community, as well as attracting tons of writers, photographers and the obligatory artists that fill up the city's cafés. A good area for pop-up shops and bars with a bit of edge.

SHOPPING

WOOD WOOD

Rochstrasse 4, 10178 Berlin
(+49 30 28047877; www.woodwood.dk)
Super-stylish shop that leans towards street labels, with men's and women's clothes, as well as rare books and zines.

INTERIOR SHOPPING

UBER WARENHAUS

Auguststrasse 26a, 10115 Berlin
(+49 30 66779095; www.ueber-store.de)
This concept shop takes on a different theme for its changing stock. When exploring the idea of melancholy, it sold everything from taxidermy to self-help books to bitter chocolate, alongside furniture and lighting.

GALLERY

PERES PROJECTS

Schlesische Str. 26, 10997 Berlin
(+49 30 61626962; www.peresprojects.com)
Hands down the hottest international gallery at the moment. A brilliantly curated space in Kreuzberg, with shows from rising stars like Terence Koh, Agathe Snow and Mark Titchner.

COFFEE

BATEAUIVRE

Oranienstrasse 18, 10999 Berlin
(+49 30 61403659)
This Kreuzberg café and bar was named after Arthur Rimbaud's poem 'The Drunken Boat' and is busy by day and buzzing at night. The tables outside are always full of smokers watching the world go by.

FOOD

GRILL ROYAL

Friedrichstrasse 105b, 10117, Berlin
(+49 30 28879288; www.grillroyalberlin.de)
This hilariously glamorous restaurant feels straight out of a Bret Easton Ellis novel. A place to dress up and stare at celebrities, Russian oligarchs and the fashion world.

DRINK

WHITE TRASH FAST FOOD

Schönhauser Allee 6/7, Berlin
(www.whitetrashfastfood.com)
Formerly in Mitte, White Trash Fast Food is a bar, club, tattoo parlour and restaurant, with an over-the-top Chinese restaurant interior and a changing line-up of punk bands. Only in Berlin.

CLUB

COOKIES

Corner of Friedrichstrasse and Unter den Linden Mitte, 10119 Berlin (+49 30 27492940; www.cookies.ch)
Rather glam (by Berlin standards) house and techno club, with multiple dance floors and a cool crowd. Topped by Cookies Cream – a sexy, white cube restaurant.

HOTEL

OSTEL

Wriezener Karree 5, 10243 Berlin
(+49 30 25768660; www.ostel.eu)
This amusing and exceptionally cheap hotel in Berlin is themed around the former East Germany. The rooms and dormitories are filled with authentic GDR design pieces in signature oranges and browns. A retro take on rest.

London

AREA

BROADWAY MARKET

East London has been the heart of London's creative world for over a decade now. Those in the know are moving away from the East's old stomping ground of Shoreditch, a.k.a. Hoxton, and going farther east into the borough of Hackney for the best galleries, cafés, bars and odd shops.

SHOPPING

DOVER STREET MARKET

17–18 Dover Street, London W1S 4LT
(+44 20 7518 0680; www.doverstreetmarket.com)
This Commes des Garçons multi-label store in Mayfair sells high fashion, rare books and strange taxidermy, amid a changing setting of art installations. Stop off at the Rose Bakery for cake on the fourth floor.

INTERIOR SHOPPING

SHELF

40 Cheshire Street, London E2 6EH
(+44 20 7739 9444; www.helpyourshelf.co.uk)
A great shop off Brick Lane for creative gifts and interior odds and ends.

GALLERY

STUART SHAVE MODERN ART

23–25 Eastcastle Street, London, W1W 8DF
(+44 20 7299 7950; www.stuartshavemodernart.com)
Cult East End space that stills impresses from its new home off Oxford Street. The place to see edgier artists like Steven Shearer, Nigel Cooke and Ed Templeton.

COFFEE

MAISON BERTAUX

28 Greek Street, London W1 5DQ
(+44 20 7437 6007)
This deco French café in Soho makes the best croissants in London and is always filled with the fashion world. It also has a brilliant women's boutique hidden in the basement.

FOOD

BISTROTHEQUE

23–27 Wadeson Street, London E2 9DR
(+44 20 8983 7900; www.bistrotheque.com)
This Hackney restaurant has a classic British menu and is surprisingly popular considering its location. There is also a camp cabaret room and a popular cocktail bar on the ground floor.

DRINK

THE GRIFFIN

93 Leonard Street, London EC2A 4RD
(+44 20 7739 6719)
This cool, but totally unpretentious pub, is true London. The worn-out narrow pub has a pool table at the back, changing DJs and a hidden gallery behind the bar.

CLUB

SMASH & GRAB AT PUNK

14 Soho Street, London W1D 3DN
(www.myspace.com/smashandgrabclub)
London's club life is notoriously fickle. The best way to find something hot is not to stick to venues but check dirtydirtydancing.com for photos of the carnage. Veteran girl duo The Queens of Noize always attract dirty celebrities at their weekly in Soho.

HOTEL

ANDAZ

40 Liverpool Street, London EC2M 7QN
(+44 20 7961 1234; www.andaz.com)
Formerly the Great Eastern Hotel, this sexy hotel puts on book and club events, art shows and is the best location to stumble back to after east London party nights.

New York

AREA
LOWER EAST SIDE

Although Manhattan's gentrification continues, the Lower East Side still has some gritty urban edge. The streets around Rivington, Orchard and Ludlow are filled with skaters, models, artists, musicians and anyone else who defines themselves as cool.

SHOPPING
NORTHSIDE JUNK

197 North 9th Street, corner of Driggs Avenue, Williamsburg, Brooklyn 11211
(www.myspace.com/northsidejunk)
This chaotic store in Brooklyn lies somewhere between a fleapit and an antique shop. Everything is crammed into this insane space – records, clothes, worn 1980s toys and general junk.

INTERIOR SHOPPING
PAULA RUBENSTEIN LTD

65 Prince Street, New York 10012
(+1 212 966 8954)
This shop off Broadway in Soho is a brilliant find, filled with odd antiques and retro goodies, from prison memorabilia to wooden alphabet blocks.

GALLERY
DEITCH PROJECTS

76 Grand Street and 18 Wooster Street, New York 10013
(+1 212 343 7300; www.deitch.com)
The place to see hot underground artists who are breaking into the mainstream, including Steve Powers, Chris Johanson, Barry McGee, Os Gemeos and Swoon.

COFFEE
BROWN

61 Hester Street, between Essex Street and Ludlow Street, New York 10002
(+1 212 477 2427; www.greenbrownorange.com)
This café–restaurant in the Lower East Side has everything you'd want for a coffee – a rustic wooden interior, big windows to stare at passers-by, and the best coffee and brunch in the city.

FOOD
CAFÉ HABANA

17 Prince Street at Elizabeth Street, New York 10012
(+1 212 625 2002)
Hip New Yorkers love their Mexican food, and this daytime spot is rammed with people diving into some of the city's best (and most reasonable).

DRINK
MAX FISH

178 Ludlow Street, New York 10002
(www.maxfish.com)
An underground institution on the Lower East Side. This grimy venue has a pool table, seriously large measures of alcohol and an amazing jukebox (when it works…).

CLUB
APT

419 West 13th Street, New York 10014
(+1 212 414 4245; www.aptwebsite.com)
A laid-back, hip club in the West Village for the cream of hip hop, soul and good conversation.

HOTEL
HOTEL ON RIVINGTON

7 Rivington Street, New York 10002
(+1 212 475 2600; www.hotelonrivington.com)
You could not be more central than a hotel in the middle of the Lower East Side. A very slick, modern and stylish hotel, with a sexy restaurant and lounge.

Paris

AREA
CANAL SAINT-MARTIN

Paris's idea of creative and hip is still pretty beautiful and glamorous compared to most cities. There are cool bars along the canal and lively restaurants in side streets nearby. In the summer, everyone grabs a spot on the Quai de Valmy for waterside picnics.

SHOPPING
COLETTE

213 rue Saint-Honoré, 75001 Paris
(www.colette.fr)

This destination store sells everything from underground zines to chic geek technology, to super-expensive clothing. The changing exhibitions and over-the-top water bar are also worth a peek.

INTERIOR SHOPPING
LES PUCES DE SAINT-OUEN PORTE DE CLIGNANCOURT

It would be daft not to mention the biggest flea market in the world, at the Porte de Clignancourt. An Aladdin's cave of objects (with more than forty thieves; be warned).

GALLERY
YVON LAMBERT

108 rue Vieille du Temple, 75003 Paris
(+33 1 42 71 09 33; www.yvon-lambert.com)

A top-notch art space in an area peppered with smaller galleries. Check out the affiliated bookshop, with its limited-edition art pieces by international big names.

COFFEE
CHEZ PRUNE

71 Quai de Valmy, 75010 Paris
(+33 1 42 41 30 47)

A buzzing café bar alongside the Canal Saint-Martin. The lucky few grab the in-demand tables outside.

FOOD
TOKYO EAT AT PALAIS DE TOKYO

13 avenue de Président Wilson, 75116 Paris
(+33 1 47 20 00 29; www.palaisdetokyo.com)

This high-design restaurant inside the cavernous modern art gallery, Palais de Tokyo, is a very fashionable world food spot, with chairs by Zevs, lamps by Stephane Maupin and tables by Ivan Fayard.

DRINK
LA PERLE

78 rue Vieille du Temple, 75003 Paris
(+33 1 42 72 69 93)

This café-bar in the Marais with an ageing 1970s interior is rammed with the creatives lining up for beers and kirs. Good for a shot of café noir in the daytime, too.

CLUB
LE PARIS PARIS

5 avenue de l'Opéra, 75002 Paris
(www.leparisparis.com)

The oh-so-cool club where people behind Ed Banger records and edgy celebrities dance to electro and drink cocktails in a black and neon interior.

HOTEL
HOTEL AMOUR

8 rue Navarin, 75009 Paris
(+33 1 48 78 31 80; www.hotelamour.com)

Another branch of graffiti artist André's international cool empire. A reasonable Pigalle hotel with rooms decorated by artists including M/M, Sophie Calle and André himself.

Tokyo

AREA
NAKAMEGURO

This relaxed, low-rise area south of Shibuya is based around a river lined by cherry blossom trees. A stylish place filled with low-key design shops, small boutiques and cool cafés.

SHOPPING
DELFONICS

Omotesando Hills B3F, 4-12-10 Jingumae, Shibuya-ku, Tokyo, 150-0001 (+81 3 5410 0590; www.delfonics.com)

This brand infuses stationary with emotion. A stunning rainbow of the best paper, notebooks and photo albums emblazoned with poetic sentences. There's also a great branch in the basement of department store Parco.

INTERIOR SHOPPING
D&DEPARTMENT PROJECT

8-3-2, Okusawa, Setagaya-ku, Tokyo 158-0083 (www.d-department.jp)

A great interiors shop that sells new and refurbished furniture. They also created the 60VISION product line, reissuing classic 1960s Japanese design classics.

GALLERY
TOKYO WONDER SITE

1-19-8 Jinnan Shibuya-ku, Tokyo 150-0041 (+81 3 3463 0603; www.tokyo-ws.org)

This art space specializes in supporting new artists, and holds creative events and talks. It also has a small but lively bar and restaurant attached.

COFFEE
BAPE CAFÉ

B1F, 5-3-18 Minami-Aoyama, Minato-ku, Tokyo 150-001 (+81 3 5778 9726; www.bape.com)

The café branch of Nigo's streetwear empire. This super-cool place is covered in KAWS paintings and Bape's signature ape insignia – even down to the sugar cubes.

FOOD
GONPACHI

1-13-11 Nishi-Azabu, Minato-ku, Tokyo 106-0031 (+81 3 5771 0170); E. Space Tower 3-6, Maruyama-cho Shibuya-ku, Tokyo 150-0044 (+81 3 5784 2011; www.gonpachi.jp)

This buzzing Ikyzaka restaurant in Roppongi was allegedly the inspiration for the restaurant in *Kill Bill*. There's also a less touristy branch in Shibuya for a clubbier music crowd.

DRINK
SUPERDELUXE

B1F 3.1.25 Nishi Azabu, Minato-ku, Tokyo 106-0031 (+81 3 5412 0515; www.super-deluxe.com)

This very cool bar in Roppongi puts on an awesome selection of events and music nights, including popular creative networking showcase Pecha Kucha.

CLUB
LE BARON

Aoyama Center Bldf B1F 3.8.40, Minami-Aoyama, Minato-ku, Tokyo 107-0062 (+81 3 3408 3665; www.lebaron.jp)

Much larger than the French club it is based on, this spot has a Daft Punk-style red light and velvet interior. It attracts international and Japanese cool kids and is the best club in the city.

HOTEL
TOKYO PARK HYATT

3-7-1-2 Nishi-Shinjuku, Shinjuku-ku, Tokyo 163-1055 (+81 3 5322 1234; www.tokyo.park.hyatt.com)

The star of *Lost in Translation* is not only the best hotel in Tokyo, it may be the best in the world. Everything is perfect – the service, the spa, the views, the food. Non-guests also flock to the jazz bar on the 55th floor.

ACKNOW-LEDGE-MENTS

This book was an enormous endeavour. The process was very word-of-mouth, and I want to thank the many kind people around the globe who helped me with recommendations. I want to thank firstly all the people who let me into their homes. Heartfelt thanks to the many people I visited who didn't make the final cut. Plus thanks to Aiko at Bape, Alexandre Senes, Alexis Zavialoff, Ana Finel Honigman, Daniel West, Donald Dinwiddie, Fleur Britten, Helen Evans, Ithai Goldberg, Javier Peres, Junsuke, Sakiko, all at *Dazed* Japan, Kate van den Boogert, Kris Latocha, Lindsey Dupler, Lotje Sodderland, Mai Miyazaki at Kaikai Kiki, Maxjet, Nadege Winter, Naoko Higashi for her invaluable help in Tokyo, Nathan Nedorostek, Paola Gavin, Paul McDevitt, Pavia Rosati, Ku' Damm 101 Hotel in Berlin, Q Hotel in Berlin, Riflemaker Gallery, Ryan Giese and Shanny, Seana Gavin, The German Tourist Board, The Grand Hyatt Tokyo, The Hotel Ginza Seiyo, Tiffany Noe, Tokyo Park Hyatt, Trevor Jackson, Wes Lang, Yoske Nishiumi and, of course, Andy Sewell. This book is dedicated to my inspirational sister Bianca – because it's her turn.